DiSCUSSiON MANUAL for STUDENT DiSCIPLESHiP

Evangelism is on the increase all over the world. Thousands of people are responding to the claims of Jesus Christ, and are finding new life in Him.

Studies show that nearly 95% of those who receive Christ as Saviour do so before they reach age 21. Because of this, great numbers of Christian babies (spiritually) are in need of <u>solid</u> spiritual growth.

Therefore, the pressure on the existing Christian community to do meaningful discipleship among young believers is becoming more intense. It is because of this growing need that this discipleship manual was conceived, written and published.

It is in this sense that the authors offer their contribution of this manual. In no way is it felt that this material is discipleship's "final word." It is hoped that this material, in its simplicity, will help you as you seek to obey God's command to "...feed my sheep."

Dawson McAllister is an intense, dynamic youth speaker who has a deep love for the young and their spiritual growth.

Speaking in The Student Relationships Conferences, classrooms, assemblies, and in churches, Dawson has met thousands of teenagers and young adults all over the United States.

Believing that there is probably no greater need today than for careful follow-up on those who accept Christ at a young age, Dawson developed the "Discussion Manual for Student Discipleship" with associates Dan Webster and Jim Lamb.

Dawson is a graduate of Bethel College in St. Paul, Minnesota and attended Talbot Seminary in LaMirada, California.

Dan Webster has been active in meeting the needs of hundreds of teenagers as a youth worker at Garden Grove Community Church in Garden Grove, California. It is here, in this huge suburban church, that Dan is able to see which methods are really effective in making Biblical principles real to kids on a day-to-day, year-by-year context.

He is a graduate of Cypress College (Calif.) and of Biola College in Los Angeles. Dan draws the insights that are reflected in this material from personal involvement in helping his young people solve spiritual growth problems with success.

INSTRUCTIONS

USE OF THE MATERIAL

Many students and young believers are reluctant
to read material that is simply given to them. For
this reason, this <u>Discussion Manual for Student
Discipleship</u> shouldn't be handed out like a booklet
or a gospel tract.

However, a young believer will learn much when a
caring (and careful) Christian takes that new one
through this material. It is designed to be used
in a reading/sharing manner.

Any person discipling a young believer should be
prepared to sit down and go over the material with
that person. It would be well worth the effort of
such a Christian guide to become familiar with this
manual's contents before attempting to lead anyone
through its pages.

QUESTIONS IN THE MATERIAL

There were two essential purposes in the authors'
minds in the selection, style and placement of the
questions in the manual.

First, the questions are asked to provoke users
to meaningful thought and discussion. Such deeper
encounters may be more helpful to the new Christian
than all the rest of the material in a specific time
between younger and older believers.

Second, the questions are obviously used in some
places to bring out a point, or to make Scripture
clearer to the student. While some questions

may seem simplistic, it is our experience that it is next to impossible to make spiritual truths too easy.

THE ART*

The material's cartoon/illustrations were selected for <u>visual</u> <u>focus</u> on spiritual truth. Designed and placed for this purpose, they should be used by the guide for discussion assistance. Make sure that the new believer takes a long look at the artwork.

MATERIAL PLACEMENT

Each discussion builds on the preceding material. In some ways the manual gets "deeper," so it would be wise to stay with this intended progression. It is encouraged that exception be taken to this advice if a specific need can be met by directing the young believer to a specific discussion.

CONTENTS

The importance of
YOUR NEW LIFE
DiSCUSSioN 1

THE BiG DECiSioN.

You made a decision awhile ago, when you accepted
Jesus Christ into your heart and life. But think
for a moment about...

- what decision you made
- what happened when you made that decision
- what attitude changes have resulted in your life
  (The very fact that you are willing to do this
  self-examining shows that God is working in you)

Do you have any questions so far?

The two main questions to ask yourself now are:

1. What happened when you received Christ?

2. Will Jesus ever leave you?

Here's what the Bible says about what happened to you when you asked Jesus Christ into your life...

Revelation 3:20
"Jesus said, 'Behold, I stand at the door and knock; if anyone hears My voice and opens the door, <u>I will come in to him</u>, and will <u>dine with him, and he with Me</u>.'"

1. When did Christ knock at the door of your life?

_____

_____

2. Because you heard the voice and you opened the door of your life that day, what does Christ say He did for you? _____

_____

3. If you have asked Christ into your life, where is He right now? _____

4. When He said He would come in to your life do you think He would trick or deceive you?

_____

5. What are you using for your basis of authority when you answer these questions? _____

Now that you have let Jesus Christ into your very innermost being, you have started a NEW LIFE of believing and trusting in Him.

What does this NEW LIFE mean to you?

II Corinthians 5:17
"Therefore if any man is in Christ, he is a new creature; the old things passed away; behold, new things have come."

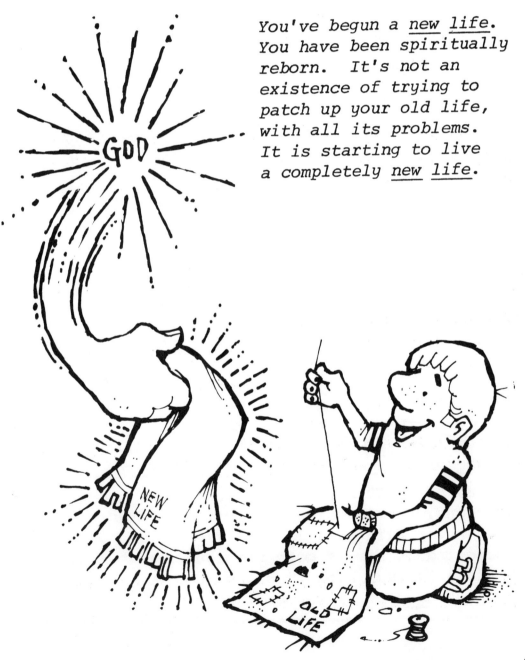

You've begun a new life. You have been spiritually reborn. It's not an existence of trying to patch up your old life, with all its problems. It is starting to live a completely new life.

This _new_ _life_ consists of believing in Him...

John 7:38
"He who believes in Me, as the Scripture said,
'From his innermost being shall flow rivers of
living water.'"

Does Christ promise this abundant and meaningful
new _life_ deep within your innermost being if you
believe in Him? (Yes)

What does it mean to believe? _____

_____

BETTER THAN A FRIEND.

Believing in Christ is almost like believing in
a friend, and learning to trust Him. (But Christ
will never fail you, like a friend can.) And
believing in Him is more than just an emotional
or intellectual commitment, as you now know.
It means _action_ -- a commitment of your will.

As a person in whom Christ now lives, you'll want to understand three important concepts, which are the ingredients of your new life. These concepts are FACT, FAITH, and FEELING. --- And it's good to know how you should relate them to each other!

I. Fact

The Bible is the Word of God. In it you find the
FACTS in which you base your FAITH and your FEELING.
These include the birth, death, and resurrection
of Jesus.

II. Faith

You base your FAITH in these FACTS from God's Word.
(Faith not based on these facts is without meaning.)
So you read the historical and spiritual truth of
the Bible and rest your FAITH in that truth, knowing
that _God_ _never_ _lies_!

III. Feeling

FEELINGS are part of your new life in Jesus Christ.
When your feelings even make you _doubt_ that you're
really God's child, "take" your feelings back to
the FACTS of God's Word and _bury_ them in His truth!.

I. FACT

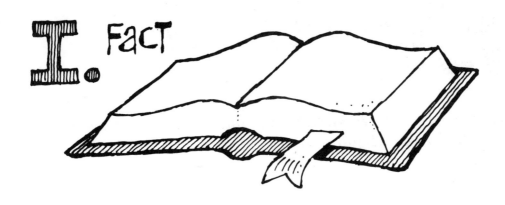

II. FAITH

III. FEELING

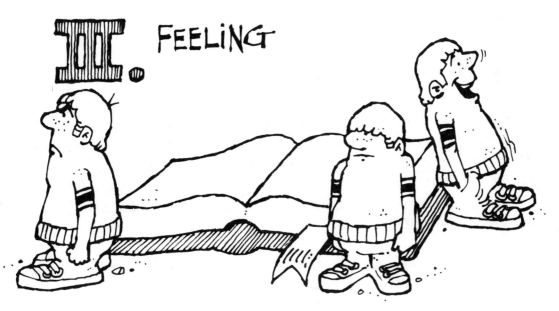

WiLL JeSus Christ eveR Leave You?

Now that Jesus Christ is in your life, <u>do you think there would ever come a time when He'd leave you?</u>

God wants you to <u>KNOW</u> that under no circumstances will He <u>ever</u> <u>leave</u> you!!!

I John 5:11-13
"And the witness is this, that God has given us <u>eternal</u> <u>life</u>, and this life is in His Son. He who has the Son <u>has</u> <u>the</u> <u>life</u>; he who does not have the Son of God does not have the life. These things <u>I</u> <u>have</u> <u>written</u> <u>to</u> <u>you</u> <u>who</u> <u>believe</u> <u>in</u> <u>the</u> <u>name</u> <u>of</u> <u>the</u> <u>Son</u> <u>of</u> <u>God</u>, <u>in</u> <u>order</u> that <u>YOU</u> <u>MAY</u> <u>KNOW</u> that <u>YOU</u> <u>HAVE</u> <u>eternal</u> <u>life</u>."

Already in our presentation, we have established that you, as a child of God, have Jesus (the Son) and that you also have NEW LIFE.

1. What kind of life is this? _____

2. According to verse 13 (above), does God want you to be confused as to where you stand in relation to this eternal life? _____

God says that you can KNOW that you have eternal life because Jesus promised that He would never leave you and <u>He</u> <u>never</u> <u>lies</u>!

John 10: 27-29
"<u>MY</u> sheep <u>hear</u> <u>MY</u> <u>voice</u>, and <u>I</u> <u>know</u> <u>them</u>, and <u>they</u> <u>follow</u> <u>ME</u>; and I <u>GIVE ETERNAL LIFE</u> to them; and they <u>shall</u> <u>never</u> <u>perish</u>; and <u>NO ONE</u> <u>shall</u> <u>snatch</u> <u>them</u> <u>out</u> <u>of</u> <u>MY</u> <u>hand</u>. MY Father, Who has given them to Me, is greater than all; and no one is able to snatch them out of the Father's hand."

Christ compares those who follow Him to sheep. According to verse 27 (above), three things happen to those who believe in Him. Jesus says his sheep...

A. *"HEAR MY VOICE"*
(Is it not true that you are now, more than
ever, concerned about what Jesus has to say
to you through His word?)

B. *"KNOW ME"*
(God knows you <u>completely</u> inside and out, and
still loves you!)

C. *"FOLLOW ME"*
(Is it not true that since you now belong to
Jesus, you are more concerned about what you
do, and have a <u>new</u> <u>desire</u> to please Him?)

According to verse 28 (above), Christ promises you
three things...

1. <u>*"ETERNAL LIFE"*</u>
(Not just a <u>quantity</u> of life but a <u>quality;</u>
an <u>abundant</u> life!)

2. *"NEVER PERISH"*
(This means you will <u>never</u> be removed from
the presence of God, once you are His!)

3. *"NO ONE SNATCHES [YOU]*
<u>*OUT OF HIS HAND"*</u>
("No one" means every
one including Satan,
friends, death, cir-
cumstances, and even
you yourself! <u>No</u>
<u>sin that you can</u>
<u>think of or commit</u>
<u>is big enough to</u>
<u>snatch you out</u>
<u>of the hands</u>
<u>of God!</u>

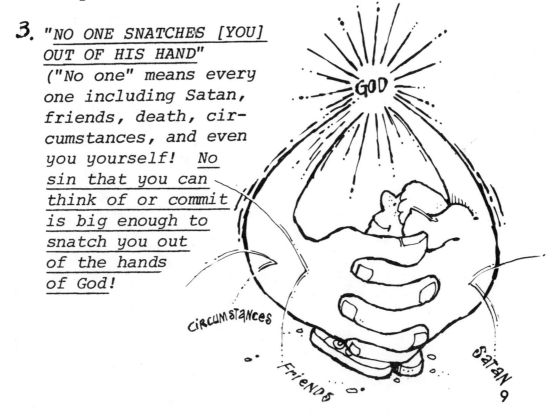

CIRCUMSTANCES

FRIENDS

SATAN

You are a child of God in much the same manner that you are related to your earthly parents. You may _say_ that you are not related to your earthly parents and you may even _feel_ that you are not related to them. You may even _change your name_, but you are still their child. In your new life with God, you are _always_ His child, and thus He has His arm around you...

Jesus says in Hebrews 13:5 that "I will never desert you, nor will I ever forsake you." Since all of your future sins have already been paid for at the cross, there is this promise by your Lord Jesus Christ that He will _always_ be with you! Perhaps you would like to thank Him right now for the fact that He'll never leave you --His child!

●THESE VERSES ARE WORTH LOOKING UP IN YOUR BIBLE:
Philippians 1:6 & 2:12,13   John 6:37-40
John 5:24   Romans 8:35-39
Ephesians 1:13

"QUIET TIME HELPS"
RELATED TO
YOUR NEW LIFE

WHAT THE QUIET TIME HELPS ARE ALL ABOUT

Every Christian needs to get quiet before God and take time to study the Bible--and worship God through prayer and praise.

After each discussion in this manual there are three "Quiet Time helps" which are designed to help you grow as a Christian.

It should take no more than a week for you to work your way through the three Quiet Time helps per discussion. After completing the three lessons you should sit down and discuss them with the person who is assisting you with the Discussion Manual for Student Discipleship.

NEW LiFE QUiET TiME 1

SUBJECT: <u>NEWNESS</u> <u>OF</u> <u>LIFE</u> <u>IN</u> <u>CHRIST</u>

Read Ezekiel 36:25-28

Questions to answer from the passage:

What does God say He will do for you when you believe in Him? _____

_____

_____

*Which of these gifts is the most meaningful to you as a Christian?*_____

_____

*Why would you say that this gift is the most meaningful to you?*_____

_____

_____

_____

What does the word <u>new</u> mean to you? My definition of new is: _____

_____

_____

_____

_____

List three new items that you have purchased or received in the last month and record common traits of newness they all have:

    1._____

    2._____

    3._____

    _____   _____

    _____   _____

    _____   _____

Turn to II Corinthians 5:17

> *Questions to answer from the passage:*

*If you believe in Christ, what has God already done for you?*_____

_____

_____

*What is the difference between a rebuilt automobile engine and a new automobile engine? (If you don't know, ask someone who would--like your father or guy at the gas station.)*_____

_____

_____

_____

*Has God given you a new heart and life or a rebuilt heart and life?*_____

_____

*Why is the answer to the previous question important?*_____

_____

_____

_____

Reread Ezekiel 36:25-28

> *Using this passage as an inspiration, write a prayer thanking God for the things He has told you that He has done for you.*

_____

_____

_____

_____

_____

_____

Now that you have written your prayer thanking God for the things He has told you that He has done for you--

1. Share it with the Lord.

2. Read it tomorrow when you get up and before you go to bed.

3. Share it with a friend at the next discipleship class.

NEW LiFE QUiET TiME 2

SUBJECT: UNDERSTANDING FACT, FAITH, FEELING AND HOW THEY RELATE TO YOUR
           CHRISTIAN WALK.

Read John 4:46-53 and re-read pages six and seven of Chapter One in the
Discipleship Manual. (Side Note: Cana of Galilee is about 20 miles from
Capernaum.)

Questions to answer from the passage:

What do you think the royal official's "feelings" were like before
he came to Jesus? (Do you think he was happy, sad, depressed or
what?) _____

_____

_____

How do you think the royal official felt between verse 50 and verse 51?

_____

_____

_____

What changes do you think occured in the royal official's feelings in
verse 51?_____

_____

_____

Was the royal official's son's healing dependent upon the man's faith or feelings? _____

_____

_____

What verse do you give to back up your conclusions? _____

_____

_____

_____

_____

_____

_____

What fact did the royal official put his faith in? _____

_____

_____ *What verse is it in?* _____

What do you think is the difference between the royal officials "belief" in verse 50 and his "belief" in verse 53? _____

_____

_____

_____

_____

_____

_____

_____

_____

_____

_____

_____

On the lines below record what you think are the different aspects of the royal officials faith and feeling from the time he encountered Jesus to the time he found out his son was healed.

	BEFORE HEALING	BETWEEN TIME	AFTER HEALING
F	_____	_____	_____
E	_____	_____	_____
E			
L	_____	_____	_____
I			
N	_____	_____	_____
G			
S	_____	_____	_____

****

F	_____	_____	_____
A	_____	_____	_____
I			
T	_____	_____	_____
H			
	_____	_____	_____

How important are "our feelings" as they relate to our Christian life?

_____

_____

_____

Is God's work in your life dependent upon them? _____

_____

_____

_____

_____

NEW LIFE QUIET TIME 3

SUBJECT: <u>THE SENSITIVITY OF JESUS TO THE NEEDS OF PEOPLE AND HIS ABILITY
TO MEET THEM.</u>

Read John 5:1-9, 14

>   *Jesus is interested in people as individuals. He is desirous
>   and capable of meeting the needs of those who look to Him.
>   From the encounter that Jesus had with this sick man, answer
>   the following questions.*

What needs do you feel this man had, other than his physical sickness?

_____

_____

_____

Do you think that this man was genuinely trying to obtain healing?___

_____

_____

_____

Why do you think this is important?_____

_____

_____

_____

_____

_____

_____

Do you think Jesus is more sensitive to those who really desire healing?

_____ *Why?* _____

_____

_____

_____

How did Jesus express His sensitivity and concern for this man before He healed him? _____

_____

_____

_____

How did Jesus carry out His sensitivity to this man in a physical way? (Be sure to check verse 14 also.) _____

_____

_____

_____

_____

_____

> *This man, and all people (including you), have basic psychological needs. They are--the need to* belong, *the need to* feel secure, *the need for* continual new experiences, *the need for* real love, *and the need for* freedom from guilt. *There are others, but this list will be enough for us.*

Which of these needs did Jesus meet in the man he healed? _____
Give the verse reference for the needs you feel Jesus met.

Belonging _____

Security _____

New Experience _____

Freedom from Guilt _____

Love _____

Concerning your needs, fill in the following chart:

How does the Lord Jesus meet these needs in your life?	How do other Christians meet these needs you have?	How can you meet these needs in other lives?
BELONGING John 1:12		
_____	_____	_____
SECURITY Matthew 28:20 Hebrews 13:5		
_____	_____	_____
NEW EXPERIENCES II Cor. 5:17 John 3:1-8		
_____	_____	_____
AFFIRMATION Matt 5:13-15		
_____	_____	_____
LOVE John 3:16		
_____	_____	_____
FREEDOM FROM GUILT Isa. 43:25, 44:22		
_____	_____	_____

On the previous page, you stated how you might meet these needs in others lives. Now that you have done that, state <u>who</u> you are going to care for, <u>when</u> you are going to do it, and <u>what</u> practically you are going to do. Also record the need you think you'll be meeting.

						WHO
						WHAT
						WHEN
						NEED

The importance of
GOD'S LOVE
AND FORGIVENESS
DISCUSSION 2

MORE THAN a "FIRE ESCAPE"

The Christian life is far more than a Sunday affair.
It is also more than a "fire escape" from hell.

As you already know, this new life with Jesus Christ
is a <u>moment-by-moment life</u>, where you talk to God and
get to know Him better in every experience *you*
have from now on.

Sometimes, because of your rebellious <u>old</u> <u>nature</u>
(which is still in you), you disobey God, and you
<u>sense that something is wrong</u>! You had been aware
of His presence and power in your life, but now it
isn't there as it was, and something is "out of whack."

<u>You have sinned against God, and you know it.</u>

So LET'S GET INTO...
- the steps to take after you have disobeyed God
- what God does when you take those steps
- your response to what God does about your sins

23

> Two things you need to remember, after you have sinned against God, are that <u>God still loves you</u> (while hating your sin), <u>and you are still His child!</u>

Your natural reaction, when you have sinned and know it, is to think that God has left you and doesn't love you anymore. But God says His very great love for you is undiminished, and you stand perfect in His presence.

The Bible says, in I John 4:8, that "<u>God is love.</u>"

What does it mean when it says, "God is love"?

_____

_____

(It means He doesn't just "have" love for you or "not have" love for you...He <u>is</u> love. His entire nature is permeated --completely soaked-- in real love. He is the <u>source</u> of love. He started it! All that is love, is God!)

LOVE is...

I Corinthians, chapter 13, defines <u>what love is</u>.

Since "all that is love is God," let's put His name in place of the word <u>love</u> as we read this chapter. <u>This will help you know more about God.</u>

(READ THE CHAPTER NOW.)

THEREFORE GOD IS <u>ALL</u>...

- patient (in the sense that only God can be)
- kind   ("   "   "   "   "   "   "   ")
- bearing of all things ("   "   "   "   ")
- hopeful of all things ("   "   "   "   ")

24

THEREFORE GOD IS NOT...

- jealous (in the sense that we can be as humans)
- bragging ("   "   "   "   "   "   "   "   "   )
- unbecoming ("   "   "   "   "   "   "   "   )
- selfish ("   "   "   "   "   "   "   "   "   )
- provoked ("   "   "   "   "   "   "   "   )
- keeping accounts ("   "   "   "   "   "   "   )

Because all these things are true, and because His love is forever, look what this means. It means it is _impossible_ to drain His love for you, _no matter what you do or fail to do as His child!_

Romans 8:38-39
"For I am convinced that neither death, nor life, nor angels, nor principalities, nor things present, nor things to come, nor powers, nor height, nor depth, nor any other created thing, shall be able to separate us from the love of God, which is in Christ Jesus our Lord."

"NOT GUILTY."

Not only is God's great love for you undiminished, but you stand before Him "not guilty"--through His acceptance of what Jesus did for you on the cross.

Romans 5:1
"Therefore having been _justified_ by faith, we have peace with God through our Lord Jesus Christ."

What does it mean to be _justified_? _____

_____

_____

The following diagram may better illustrate the concept of _justification_ for you...

GOD

HOLINESS

LOVE

JUSTICE

HOLINESS

God is absolutely holy. He cannot stand sin.
He has said that, "The wages of sin is death."

Romans 6:23

LOVE

But God also loves you. He knows that you are
His child--if, in fact, you are--even when you
sin. Sinning doesn't make God disown you.

Romans 8:38-39

JUSTICE

Now God is also just. His holiness, love, and
justice all require total, absolute satisfaction
in order for you to become His child.

This situation was why He sent Jesus Christ.
He came and bore all of your wrongness (sin)
on Himself, and then defeated that sin.

God won't sidestep an issue or rationalize sin.
It has to be paid for and it was, on the cross
of Jesus. Now, when God looks at you, He sees
you with your awful sin bill already paid!

This is possible because He sees you wrapped in
the perfectness of Jesus Christ, your Saviour.
He accepts you because of what Christ did on
the cross, AS THOUGH YOU HAD NEVER SINNED!

BUT...

> ...You need to know that, when you sin, you deeply hurt God. You need to agree (confess) with Him that you have been wrong and want to change from your old ways, patterns, and habits.

Did you know that you could hurt God deeply?

Ephesians 4:30
"And do not grieve the Holy Spirit of God, by whom you were sealed for the day of redemption."

What does grieve mean? _____

(Deeply hurt.)

What sins do you do that can hurt God's very Spirit?

_____

Even though you're in God's family, you can still hurt Him. Which hurts you more --when a stranger tells you, "You'll never amount to anything," or when a person close to you tells you that?

In the same way, when you tell God His love doesn't amount to much, His power isn't too much, His wisdom isn't much, then you hurt Him more than any non-Christian can by saying, "God doesn't exist." Though God still loves you, your fellowship with Him is hampered.

Psalms 66:18
"If I regard wickedness in my heart, the Lord will not hear...."

28

> It is necessary for you to confess your sins to God when you sin as His child. Unhampered fellowship will be restored when you do.

I John 1:9
"If we <u>confess</u> our sins, He is faithful and just to forgive us our sins and to cleanse us from <u>all</u> unrighteousness."

When you truly understand what <u>your</u> <u>sin</u> has done to God, to others, and to yourself, you will have the <u>true</u> <u>sorrow</u> that leads to confession and change.

What does it mean to confess your sins?_____

_____ 29

Confession involves three things...

- *agreeing with God that He was right, and that what you did was wrong. (This is difficult, because of pride.)*

- *agreeing with God that Christ paid for that sin in full.*

- *deciding by an act of the will that you will turn away from that wrong that so hurt God.*

> *Why is just "feeling sorry" about your sins not true confession? Because "feeling sorry" doesn't mean that you agree that Christ has taken care of it or that you have decided to quit doing that thing. "Feeling sorry" by itself only produces guilt feelings, not fellowship with God!*

When you confess your sins (according to 1 John 1:9), how much of your sin is forgiven? _____

What does all include? _____

_____

(Everything you could ever do.)

Isaiah 43:25
"I, even I, am the one who wipes out your transgressions for My own sake; and I will not remember your sins."

When you confess your sin, what does God do with your sin? _____

How can God wipe out your sin? _____

_____

(He wiped it out 2000 years ago on the cross.)

30

IMPORTANT!

> It's very important for you to remember that your sins have been wiped out.

God separates your sin TOTALLY from Himself.
possible for our imaginations, from Himself.

Psalm 103:11-12
"For as high as the heavens are above the earth, so great is His lovingkindness toward those who fear Him. As far as the east is from the west, so far has He removed our transgressions from us."

How high is the heaven above the earth?

How far is the east from the west?

Hebrews 10:17
"And their sins and their lawless deeds I will remember no more."

If God forgets your sins, can He hold them against you? _____

> SINCE GOD HAS WIPED OUT YOUR SINS, SEPARATING THEM AS FAR AS THE EAST IS FROM THE WEST, AND FORGETS THEM, THEN WHAT SHOULD BE YOUR RESPONSE TO GOD'S TOTAL FORGIVENESS?
>
> You should also forget, and be thankful. And you should realize that you are now in fellowship with God, and you should continue to live for Him.

Psalm 51:12-13
"Restore to me the joy of Thy salvation, and sustain me with a willing spirit. Then I will teach transgressors Thy ways, and sinners will be converted to Thee."

One important thing must not be forgotten. After your fellowship with God has been restored, you must restore your human fellowships. Look at the results of your sin <u>once</u> <u>more</u> before forgetting it. This is to be very honest with yourself and <u>see if this sin hurt another person</u> in any way.

If it did, go to that other person. Ask that person's <u>forgiveness of the wrong</u> done him/her and restore any loss caused to that person, if humanly possible.

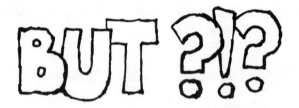

<u>What about guilt feelings?</u>

You may experience guilt feelings --<u>even</u> <u>after</u> you have confessed your sins to God and asked His forgiveness, and <u>even after</u> you have asked for forgiveness of those you may have wronged when you sinned.

These guilt feelings are from Satan. <u>Or</u>, they are caused by your own unwillingness to forget. <u>Either</u> <u>way</u>, THEY CAN'T BE FROM GOD... HE HAS ALREADY FORGOTTEN THEM!

Right now, why don't you take a piece of paper and write down the sins you have done --those which come easily into your mind again and again, and which Satan uses in his warfare against you!

After you have listed them, take God's own words in I John 1:9 and write, "I John 1:9" over the list. _Tear it up and throw it away!_

It is that simple with God when you're sincere, so remember to talk to Him and thank Him for His forgiveness!

"QUIET TIME HELPS" RELATED TO GOD'S LOVE AND FORGIVENESS

WHAT THE QUIET TIME HELPS ARE ALL ABOUT

Every Christian needs to get quiet before God and take time to study the Bible--and worship God through prayer and praise.

After each discussion in this manual there are three "Quiet Time helps" which are designed to help you grow as a Christian.

It should take no more than a week for you to work your way through the three Quiet Time helps per discussion. After completing the three lessons you should sit down and discuss them with the person who is assisting you with the Discussion Manual for Student Discipleship.

FORGIVENESS QUIET TIME 1

SUBJECT: <u>UNDERSTANDING JUSTIFICATION</u>

Why you need forgiveness and justification.

Read Romans 3:23

What is the natural desire of all people?_____

_____

Read Mark 7:21-23

"People have a problem with the condition of their heart." Do you
agree with this?_____ What does it mean?_____

_____

_____

_____

_____

Read Titus 3:3

What type of conduct are people into?_____

_____

_____

Read Romans 3:13-14

What do the words of people reflect?_____

_____

_____

Do you agree or disagree with the following quote?_____

     "The things that come out of a person's mouth only reflect
     what is in their heart."

Why do you agree or disagree?_____

_____

Sum up the problem of humanity in one or two sentences.

_____

_____

_____

*State in one or two sentences the dilemma that the conclusion
of the previous questions bring as you compare them with the
following question.*

_____

_____

_____

_____

Read Isaiah 5:16, 6:3

What one attribute of God is emphasized in these verses? _____

*Read the following quote from John Murray in his book Redemption Accomplished
and Applied. "The person who is against God cannot be right with God. For
if we are against God then God is against us. It could not be otherwise.
God cannot be indifferent to or complacent towards that which is the contra-
diction of himself. His very perfection requires the recoil of righteous
indignation. And that is God's wrath...This is our situation and it is
our relation to God; how can we be right with him?"*

Read Romans 3:23-26; 5:1

*What is the solution to the problem of humanity?*_____

_____

_____

> *Justification: The judicial act of God declaring one to be
> righteous by imputation of righteousness to
> him.   To be set right with God.*

Reread the above quote by John Murray.

*How does Romans 5:8-10 defend this quote?*_____

_____

38

Read Psalm 85:2-3 and Romans 4:8

*What does the Bible say about a person who is justified?*_____

_____

_____

PRACTICAL UNDERSTANDING--

*Have you ever loaned something to someone with the agreement that it would be returned and it wasn't?*_____ *What?*_____

*Have you ever borrowed something from someone and said that you would repay them or return it and didn't?*_____ *What?*_____

Let's say for example, that you borrowed $100 from me and signed an agreement to pay it back in ten days. Well, twenty days pass and you don't pay me back. Setting all emotional ties aside, we have a legal problem! You owe me money. I take you to court -- remember, we're dealing strictly with the law, not emotional friendship -- and the judge tells you to pay up. You say, "I don't have the money, judge." The judge then raises his gavel to pronounce sentence. At that moment, a man in the court rises and says, "Judge, I'll pay the debt for that person." The man comes forward and pays my $100 plus court expenses. The judge then says, "Court dismissed, debt paid in full!" The point is that your debt was paid, justification took place. Your debt before God is all the sin you have committed as you have broken His laws. Jesus Christ paid for it on the cross -- YOU ARE JUSTIFIED IN GOD'S SIGHT!
"You Have Been Justified. This is to say that God looks upon you and deals with you as though you were perfectly righteous, as though you had never sinned and will never sin. However difficult this idea may be for you to grasp, it represents an event that has already taken place and will never change.

"It is not that God wears blinders and pretends you are better than you are. He knows about your sin. Yet his feelings toward you and his dealings with you are based on a righteousness Christ has given you. God treats you as though you were as righteous as Jesus. You may be uncomfortable with this idea.... As the impact of it breaks over your understanding you will marvel."
Quoted from The Fight by John White page 12.

Read Romans 5:8-9

What motivated God to do this for you? _____

_____

_____

Now take a moment and review the ideas and thoughts from this lesson. Based on your thoughts, write a prayer thanking God for His Love and Forgiveness.

_____

_____

_____

_____

_____

_____

_____

_____

_____

_____

Now that you have written your prayer thanking God for His love and forgiveness--

1. *Share it with the Lord.*

2. *Read it tomorrow when you get up and before you go to bed.*

3. *Share it with a friend.*

4. *Share it with the person taking you through the discipleship series.*

FORGIVENESS QUIET TIME 2

SUBJECT: CONFESSION AND FORGIVENESS

From Chapter 2 in this Discipleship Manual, record below the three things confession involves.

1._____

2._____

3._____

Read II Samuel 11:1-5

What sin did David commit?_____

_____

The next two Psalms that you will look at and study David wrote, after his sin with Bathsheba.

Read Psalm 32

> Helpful definitions:
>
> Transgression = breaking God's commands.
>
> Iniquity = personal wickedness/gross injustice on your part.

Record on the chart below the results of not confessing your sins, and the results of confessing your sins to God:

VERSE	NOT CONFESSING	VERSE	CONFESSING

Read Psalm 51:10-12, 17

What was David's attitude as he prayed for forgiveness? _____

_____

_____

What was David's desire as he confessed? _____

_____

_____

What does God promise if you truly confess your sin? _____

_____

Psalm 34:18 _____

I John 1:9 _____

_____

_____

<u>Talk over the following question with the person taking you
through the discipleship series:</u>

Question: Do you think you should save your sins and confess them
           all at the end of the day; or, should you confess them
           soon after you commit them? Why?

Record one <u>new</u> thing you have learned from this study. _____

_____

FORGiVENESS QUiET TiME 3
SUBJECT: _GUILT_ _AND_ _GUILT_ _FEELINGS_

> Definition of guilt = A violation of the law involving
> a penalty to be due.

Those who break the law are legally guilty for breaking that law. When you sin -- break God's law -- you are guilty. You may, or may not, feel guilty for breaking the law. Christ's death frees you from your legal guilt before God -- He has declared you "not guilty." Review Chapter Two, Quiet Time One, for the truth of this. The enemy often uses "guilt feelings" as his weapon against God's children.

If you were going to break a chain, which link would you work on (attack)? _____

_____

_____

You would attack the weakest link, of course. This is Satan's tactic, and the area of guilt is one of the weakest links in the Christian life because of his/her still active sin nature.

Do you think God set us free from sin just to have us live a life full of guilt? _____

Read Isaiah 43:25 and II Corinthians 5:19,21

What is God's attitude toward you? _____

_____

_____

Does the fact that you are a sinner change His attitude? _____

_____

Using a concordance or footnote in your Bible, find one other verse that would support this truth.

_____

_____

_____

Guilt feelings have a tremendous effect upon Christians. They have a tendency
to immobilize the Christian and make him/her self-centered because it magnifies
their inadequacy to live the Christian lifestyle.

Read Colossians 1:22

What _has_ God done to set you free from this guilt problem? _____

_____

_____

Record your personal thoughts concerning this verse. In your own words,
how does it relate to guilt feelings?

_____

_____

_____

_____

_____

_____

_____

_____

_____

_____

_____

_____

_____

You should remember that you do feel sorrow concerning your sin, but once
you confess that sin, God no longer wants you to feel guilty.

Read II Corinthians 7:9

What should you do with the guilt feelings that you have if you have confessed your sin? _____

_____

_____

_____

What did Paul find joy in? _____

_____

_____

_____

SUMMARY: *Remember, Jesus died for your sins. He took the guilt for them. You need not feel guilty for them but direct the sorrowfulness of your sin back to God in the form of repentance.*

Read 1 John 1:9 and 2:1-2

Write God a letter thanking Him for what you have learned. Record in this letter what new truths you have learned.

_____

_____

_____

_____

_____

_____

_____

_____

_____

_____

_____

The importance of
YOUR TRIALS
Discussion 3

THiNK ABOUT SOMETHiNG FOR a MiNUTE...

✝ When you came to Christ, did all of your problems disappear?

✝ What problems (trials) are you facing right now?

✝ Do you think that God has a hand in these trials?

✝ Do problems make you want to quit the Christian life, or do they draw you closer to God?

> One of the most troubling experiences you can go through as a new Christian is to encounter a real trial or problem in your life.

Many make the mistake of thinking that the Christian life will be a bed of roses without the thorns. Speaking to a group of young Christians, Peter said,

1 Peter 4:12
"Beloved, do not be surprised at the fiery ordeal among you, which comes upon you for your testing, as though some strange thing were happening to you."

Looking at Trials...

Take a look at what some of these trials can be, how God uses them in your life, and then consider what your response should be to these trials.

Trial =

...those problems that arise from forces outside ourselves, that affect our lives, and yet catch us powerless to do anything to change the situation which results. They are a tryout to test quality, value or usefulness.

●What are some trials you might encounter?

1. You might encounter school problems (like a difficult subject or paper).

2. You might encounter people who misunderstand you because of your faith in Jesus Christ and don't like you because of your witness

3. You might experience financial problems

4. You might encounter social problems

5. *You might experience physical pain that you do not understand the reasons for*

Think of some of the problems you're facing right now...

Please list them:

1)_____

2)_____

3)_____

_____

_____

WHY DOES GOD ALLOW TRIALS?

James 1:2-4
"Consider it all joy, my brethren, when you encounter
various trials, knowing that <u>the testing of your
faith produces endurance</u>. And let endurance have its
perfect result, <u>that you may be perfect and complete,
lacking in nothing</u>."

Now, again, why does God allow trials? _____

_____

(To test our faith.)

BITING THE BULLET.

<u>God wants to have you get down to the "gritty" of your
true belief in Him. It is one thing to say you love
Jesus and believe in God. It is another to trust
Him when you are surrounded by trials. God wants to
know that you will trust Him, even when you think your
whole world is crumbling down around you.</u>

According to the verses in James (above), what kind of faith is God looking for? _____

(Enduring faith.)

> God is looking for faith in you that keeps on keeping on and keeps believing Him <u>in</u> <u>spite</u> of what happens.

- How does a track man build endurance into his body?

- How does a weight lifter become strong?

- How does a great mind develop the ability to think?

THE PRESSURE COOKER GETS RESULTS!

<u>People from all these areas of life endure pressure in order to develop the attributes (qualities) they desire in their lives. God, in the same manner, applies the pressure in your life to develop strong trust in Him.</u>

OUR RESPONSE!

James 1:2
"Consider it <u>all</u> <u>joy</u>, my brethren, when you encounter various trials..."

How should you respond to trials?_____

_____

(With all joy.)

Why should you do this?_____

_____

_____

51

*(Because a trial coming into your life brings with it
something for your own good. God has sent this trial,
whatever it is, to make you a person who is able to
trust Him in a deeper way. The finished product is
what you can have joy over, not the trial itself.*

*Why are you hurting God when you grumble under the
pressure of a trial?* _____

_____

*(Because in the grumbling, you are telling God that
He doesn't know what is best for you.)*

James 1:5
*"But if any of you lacks wisdom, let him ask of
God, who gives to all men generously and without
reproach, and it will be given to him."*

*When a trial strikes, it is easy for you to become
bankrupt of wisdom.*

* WHAT iS WiSDOM ?

> *Wisdom is the ability to see life
> and its problems from God's
> perspective.*

● *According to James 1:5, what are you to do when you
don't understand your problems?*

● *Will God hold back on His generosity when you ask?*

● *What is the verse referring to when it says God
will give without reproach?* _____

_____

*(God will not put you down. He will not embarrass you.
Even if you don't understand your trials, He will not
call you stupid. He only wants you to trust Him completely in all of life's circumstances.)*

52

GO BACK TO THE BEGINNING...

At this point, return to your list of problems now being faced (at the beginning of this discussion). Commit these problems to God. Trust that He knows what is best for you, because He _does_. _Thank_ _Him_ _for_ _these_ _trials_, believing that He will work in your life to bring you to a deeper trust in Him.

I Thessalonians 5:18
"...in everything give thanks; for this is God's will for you in Christ Jesus."

"QUIET TIME HELPS" RELATED TO YOUR QUIET TIME

WHAT THE QUIET TIME HELPS ARE ALL ABOUT

Every Christian needs to get quiet before God and take time to study the Bible--and worship God through prayer and praise.

After each discussion in this manual there are three "Quiet Time helps" which are designed to help you grow as a Christian.

It should take no more than a week for you to work your way through the three Quiet Time helps per discussion. After completing the three lessons you should sit down and discuss them with the person who is assisting you with the Discussion Manual for Student Discipleship.

TRIALS QUIET TIME 1

SUBJECT: THE PURPOSE OF TRIALS

or

The things that are hassling you now are not meant to make life miserable but to cause you to grow.

Read Romans 5:3-5

What does Paul tell you to exult or rejoice in? _____

_____

_____

What are the three results of trials (tribulations or sufferings)?_____

_____

_____

_____

_____

_____

From Galatians 5:22-23, what do you think are the qualities of proved character?

_____

_____

_____

_____

_____

_____

_____

_____

_____

God is primarily interested in developing your character. He wants you to become like Jesus. Romans 5:3-5 tells us that trials produce <u>character</u>. Here is an illustration that will help you understand the purpose of trials.

ILLUSTRATION

You are applying for a very important job. This job demands a very physically fit person. All your major muscles must be in top condition before you can qualify for this position. The person that gets this job must be able to:

1. *Run a mile in 5½ minutes.*
2. *Do 100 sit-ups*
3. *Do 15 pull-ups*
4. *Do 50 push-ups.*

As you look at the qualifications, you see that the only qualification you can now meet is sit-ups. Remember that this is an illustration! In order to get your other muscles in shape, you must endure conditioning that causes pain and sweat. Your reason for enduring the conditioning is to become fit and able for the job.

The purpose of trials is to make you spiritually fit, to strengthen your spiritual life. The trials you now face can help you grow in character, if you let the Lord do this through you. Different trials can work on different areas of your character.

If God's goal for you is to become more like Christ, more "loving, joyful, peaceful, patient, kind, good, gentle, faithful, and self-controlled" (Galatians 5:22-23), then trials are a great way to develop these qualities.

Think of the trials you now face. List four:

_____

_____

_____

_____

What quality could God develop in your life through these trials if you trust Him? List the trial, the quality, and how it could be developed. (The qualities are love, joy, peace, patience, kindness, goodness, gentleness, faithfulness, self-control.)

TRIAL	QUALITY	HOW IT CAN BE DEVELOPED
OVERWEIGHT	SELF-CONTROL	BY TRUSTING GOD TO DEVELOP DISCIPLINE IN MY LIFE AS I EAT LESS AND EXERCISE MORE.
NAGGING LITTLE BROTHER	PATIENCE	BY DEVELOPING PATIENCE AS I TRUST IN THE LORD TO CHANGE ME AND MY LITTLE BROTHER.

Look at the chart again and pray that God will develop character in your life as you trust Him to work through your trials.

TRIALS QUIET TIME 2

SUBJECT: _UNDERSTANDING TRIALS_

Read II Corinthians 4:7-10, 16, 17

In verse 8 and 9 Paul mentions four types of trails that he faced, what are they?

1. __affliction__   2. _____

3. _____   4. _____

Check a dictionary for definitions of what these mean.

1. __affliction__   =   persistant pain or distress

2. _____   =

3. _____   =

4. _____   =

What did Paul say concerning God's help to him in each of the four trial types?

TRIAL	GOD'S HELP BIBLE TEXT	WHAT THAT MEANS TO ME
1. affliction	"but not crushed"	God won't let me face pressure or pain beyond my capacity to handle.
2. _____	_____	_____
3. _____	_____	_____
4. _____	_____	_____

Can you think of any trials you are facing now? List four (they may be the same as Quiet Time #1 or different):

1. _____

2. _____

3. _____

4. _____

List the trial type, your trial, and God's promise concerning you on the
chart below:

TRiaL TYPE	MY TRiaL	GOD'S PROMISE
affliction	four term papers in the next six weeks.	They won't crush me. God will show me how to use time wisely and help me to concentrate. With Him I can do it.

What counsel does 2 Corinthians 4:16-18 give you in the middle
of trials? _____

_____

Take a moment now and dedicate your trial to the Lord. Ask Him to teach
you through them and to give you the strength to handle them.

TRIALS QUIET TIME 3

SUBJECT: *GOD'S UNDERSTANDING AND KNOWLEDGE OF YOU AND YOUR SITUATIONS.*

Read Psalm 139:1-18

As you read this passage, underline all the things God knows about you, then record them on the chart below.

VERSE	*WHAT HE KNOWS ABOUT YOU*
______	______________________________
______	______________________________
______	______________________________
______	______________________________
______	______________________________
______	______________________________
______	______________________________
______	______________________________
______	______________________________
______	______________________________
______	______________________________
______	______________________________
______	______________________________

Which one of these is the most meaningful to you? ______________

Why? ______________________________

____

What was David's response to this deep knowledge? (verses 14, 17, 18)

____

____

____

Realizing that God knows everything about you, how should this affect the way you understand a trial? _____

_____

_____

_____

_____

Read Isaiah 43:2
What does God promise you in the middle of a hard trial? _____

_____

_____

_____

_____

_____

Read Proverbs 3:5-8

As you continue to face your trials, what should you be doing? _____

_____

_____

_____

_____

The importance of
THE WORD
Discussion 4

> The Christian life is an exciting life
> --an adventure where you find out:

1. about yourself
2. about God
3. about what God expects of you
4. about your relationships with others
5. about the future
6. what real love is
7. how great it is to depend totally on Jesus
   Christ

WHAT HAVE YOU LEARNED?

> One can never learn enough of these things;
> because God has made these and many other vital
> subjects so deep, it will take all of eternity
> just to understand them.

> Because you are a new Christian, the
> understanding you have of these areas is
> just beginning to take hold in your life.

> 1 Peter 2:2
> "...like newborn babes, long for the <u>pure</u> <u>milk</u>
> <u>of</u> <u>the</u> <u>word</u>, that by it <u>you</u> <u>may</u> <u>grow</u> in
> respect to salvation."

1. What does God call a person who has just come
   to know Christ? ("newborn babes")

2. Why does He liken you to a newborn baby?
   (Because your relationship with God is new
   and you have just been born into this new
   life with God.)

3. As a new Christian what should you long for?
   ("the pure milk of the word")

4. What are the results of this longing?
   (Growth)

5. What happens to your physical strength if you
   do not eat for days?

6. What will happen to your spiritual strength
   if you fail to eat--that is, to feed on the
   Word of God and pray daily?

   (Each day you need to reserve a time to eat
   physical and spiritual food.)

I. God's plan for you is to study the Bible
   that you may know Him in a deeper way.
   Understanding God's Word will lead you to
   love and believe Him more.

   A. As a Christian, you need to understand that
      God has amazing insights for you to learn
      about Himself.

What do you know about the depth of God?	What do you know about man's understanding of God?
Romans 11:33 "Oh, the depth of the riches both of the wisdom and knowledge of God! How unsearchable are His judgments and unfathomable His ways!"	Romans 3:10-11 "...as it is written, 'THERE IS NONE RIGHTEOUS, NOT EVEN ONE; THERE IS NONE WHO UNDERSTANDS, THERE IS NONE WHO SEEKS FOR GOD...'"

Since God's ways are so deep and your understanding
is so shallow, God, in His love, has revealed more
of what He is like through His Word.

Man, because of sin and lack of understanding, cannot comprehend the ways of God. **2.**

1. GOD offers to man

GOD, therefore, has written man a letter (the Bible) to help him understand more about Himself... God even goes so far as to help him understand the Bible.

4. The more man understands God, the more he loves Him.

THAT IS WHY JESUS SAID:

John 14:21
"He who has My commandments and keeps them, he it is who loves Me; and he who loves Me shall be loved by My Father, and I will love him, and will disclose Myself to him."

1. Is it possible to obey His commandments without knowing them?
    (No, you must know what they are to obey them.)

2. How do you know God's commandments?
    (He has revealed them in His Word.)

3. What happens when you obey His commandments and let Jesus Christ control your life?
    (You will be loved by God and Jesus will reveal Himself to you.)

B. Not only do you understand more about God as a result of studying the Bible, but you will also love Him in a greater way.

    1. God's goal for you:

        1 Peter 1:8
        "...and though you have not seen Him, you love Him, and though you do not see Him now, but believing in Him. You get the FAITH TO BELIEVE in Christ by HEARING THE WORD.

        a. Have you ever seen Jesus Christ?
            The Bible says you can love Him even though you have not seen Him, through believing in Him. We get the FAITH TO BELIEVE in Christ by HEARING THE WORD.

Romans 10:17
"So faith comes from hearing, and hearing by the word of Christ."

68

II. *God wants you to study the Bible as a guide*
to living with Him and with man.

> Because your will is not in line with the will
> of God and His counsel you, you we need practical
> advice on how to live. God's Word provides you
> with this counsel.

II Timothy 3:16
"All Scripture is inspired by God and profitable
for TEACHING, for REPROOF, for CORRECTION, for
TRAINING IN RIGHTEOUSNESS..."

A. *This passage clearly shows that God is truly*
interested in using His Word in four areas of
your life.

1. TEACHING
There are many
paths in life
that a person
can take --some
are disastrous...
God and His Word
teach you to take
the right path.

2. Reproof

Sometimes in walking down God's path you rebel and get off the path... The Bible tells you where you have gotten off the path.

3. Correction

God corrects you through His Word and shows you how to get back on His path.

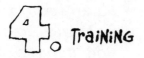

4. TRAINING

Once you get back on
the path, God does
not just leave you
there, but gives
you practical
instruction on
how to lead a
life of peace and
meaning.

B. While fads come and go as time passes, God's
   instruction, through the Bible, is always
   applicable to your life.

Mark 13:31
"Heaven and earth will pass away, but My Words
will not pass away."

1. What does Jesus say will pass away?

2. What does Jesus say will not pass away?

3. Why do you think you should spend time reading
   and obeying God's Word?
   (Because it is the eternal proven Word which
   will exist forever.)

> It would be good, at this point, for you to
> think of a time each day (even for ten minutes)
> that you could reserve for the study of God's
> Word. Think of the results of a tree planted
> by a stream. The roots of the tree go deep into
> the ground to be nourished. In the same manner,
> you need to sink your roots deep into God's Word
> so that you will grow and become strong in your
> relationship with Him.

"QUIET TIME HELPS"
RELATED TO
THE WORD

WHAT THE QUIET TIME HELPS ARE ALL ABOUT

Every Christian needs to get quiet before God and take time to study the Bible--and worship God through prayer and praise.

After each discussion in this manual there are three "Quiet Time helps" which are designed to help you grow as a Christian.

It should take no more than a week for you to work your way through the three Quiet Time helps per discussion. After completing the three lessons you should sit down and discuss them with the person who is assisting you with the Discussion Manual for Student Discipleship.

THE WORD QUIET TiME 1

SUBJECT: *THE BASICS OF THE BIBLE*

Who is the central figure of the entire Bible?

      Luke 24:44 _____

      John 5:39-47 _____

What is the name for Jesus Christ in John 1:1,14?_____

Who is considered the author of the Bible?

      Daniel 9:2 _____

      II Peter 1:20-21 _____

      Hebrews 1:5 _____

      Jeremiah 1:4,11,13 _____

What is Jesus' attitude toward Scripture?

      Matthew 24:35
      Matthew 5:17,18 _____

What is God's attitude toward Scripture?

      Isaiah 55:10,11 _____

      Jeremiah 23:28 _____

God takes notice of what type of person?

      Isaiah 66:2 _____

What part of the Bible should you base your life on?

      Proverbs 30:5,6 _____

From John's gospel, what are the results of the Word in your life?

John 8:31-32 _____

_____

John 15:3 _____

_____

John 15:7 _____

_____

John 15:11 _____

_____

John 16:33 _____

_____

John 17:17 _____

_____

What do you need in addition to God's Word to be fully equipped spiritually?

Ecclesiastes 12:11-12 _____

_____

_____

II Timothy 3:17 _____

_____

_____

THE WORD QUIET TIME 2

SUBJECT: THE IMPORTANCE OF THE BIBLE IN YOUR LIFE

The necessity of the Bible

What do the following verses say concerning the Bible and growing as a Christian?

I Peter 2:2 _____

_____

_____

Jeremiah 15:16 _____

_____

_____

Acts 20:32 _____

_____

_____

What do the following verses say concerning the Bible and overcoming sin as a Christian?

Ephesians 6:17 _____

_____

_____

I Peter 2:8 _____

_____

_____

Psalm 119:9 _____

_____

_____

What do the following verses say concerning the Bible and how it _prepares_ _you_ _to_ _serve_ _God?_

Joshua 1:8-9 _____

_____

_____

I Timothy 4:6 _____

_____

_____

II Timothy 3:16-17 _____

_____

_____

What does God promise to those who love and study the Word?

Psalm 1:1-2 _____

I Kings 2:1-3 _____

As you sit down to study the Bible, how should you prepare?

James 1:21 _____

_____

_____

I Peter 2:1-2 _____

_____

List one new truth you have learned about the Bible and yourself below:

_____

_____

_____

_____

_____

THE WORD QUIET TiME 3

Study from Psalm 119

What does the psalmist call God's Word in the following verses:

v. 1 _____
v. 2 _____
v. 3 _____
v. 4 _____
v. 5 _____
v. 6 _____
v. 7 _____
v. 43 _____
v. 72 _____
v. 91 _____
v. 123 _____

What did the psalmist find that respecting and learning God's Word resulted in?

v. 7 _____

v. 8 _____

v. 9 _____

Who are to be your companions?

v. 63 _____

Why is adversity sometimes good for you?

v. 67 _____

V. 71 _____

What value does the Word have for you?

v. 72 _____

What is necessary in order to learn the Word?

v. 73 _____

Knowing and memorizing the Word makes you...

    v. 98 _____

Meditating on the Word makes you...

    v. 99 _____

Obeying the Word makes you...

    v. 100_____

Why is this?

    v. 105_____

When does God discipline you?

    v. 126_____

What does it give you?

    v. 130 _____

How are your steps to be ordered?

    v. 133 _____

When God's Word is not kept you feel...

    v. 136_____

    v. 158_____

How can you have great peace?

    v. 165_____

The importance of
YOUR QUIET TIME
Discussion 5

When you asked Jesus Christ into your life, you began your most exciting life relationship. But did you know that the key to growth in your new relationship is in a _Quiet_ _Time_?

What is a _Quiet_ _Time_?

> All the great men and women in the Bible had a certain common trait in their lives with God.

A. These great people believed it was important to build their relationship with God. _They did this by spending time alone with Him._

Exodus 33:11
"Thus the Lord used to speak to Moses face to face, just
as a man speaks to his friend."

1. How is this great man's (Moses') fellowship
   with God described?
   (As a man speaks to his friend.)

```
+---------------------------------------------------+
| Did you know that God loves to talk with you      |
| and be your friend?  God is excited about your    |
| spending time with Him, so that you can get       |
| to know Him better as your God and friend.        |
+---------------------------------------------------+
```

Psalm 63:1a
"O God, Thou art my God, I shall seek Thee earnestly;
my soul thirsts for Thee, my flesh yearns for Thee."

1. Did this great man (David) have a desire for God?
   (Yes)

2. What did he do that he might know God better?
   (David sought after God)

   B. Even Jesus Christ, the Son of God, felt that
      it was important to spend time alone
      with His Father.

Mark 1:35
"And in the early morning, while it was still dark,
He (Jesus) arose and went out and departed to a
lonely place, and was praying there."

1. Why did Jesus get away by Himself to a quiet
   place? (So that He could pray)

2. Was it important to Jesus to spend time alone
   with His Father? (Yes)

3. How do you know it was important?
   (Because He got up early when He could have
   been sleeping)

4. Is spending time alone with God important to you?

> Jesus felt that it was so important to spend
> time with God that He sacrificed sleep in order
> to have fellowship with God.

C. Not only did the great people of the Bible
   and Jesus Christ feel it was important to
   spend time alone with God, but you are to
   have fellowship with God also.

FELLOWSHIP is close intimate sharing between two
persons. It is a two-way affair, with you speaking
to God through prayer and Him speaking to you
through His Word. God created you so that you
might have fellowship with Him.

I Corinthians 1:9
"God is faithful, through whom you were called into
fellowship with His Son, Jesus Christ our Lord."

1. *What were you called to have with Jesus Christ?*
   (Fellowship)

> There are specific reasons why
> you should spend time alone with
> God in His Word. Can you find
> these reasons in the following
> Bible verses?

Hosea 6:3 (Living Bible)
"Oh, that we might know the Lord! Let us press on
to know him, and He will respond to us as surely as
the coming of dawn or the rain of early spring."

Proverbs 3:6
"In all your ways acknowledge Him, and He will make
your path straight."

Psalm 34:4
"I sought the Lord, and He answered me, and
delivered me from all my fears."

John 15:5
"I am the vine, you are the branches; he who abides
in Me, and I in him, he bears much fruit; for apart
from Me you can do nothing."

Matthew 11:29
"Take my yoke upon you, and learn from Me, for I am
gentle and humble in heart; and you shall find rest
for your souls.

Here is a very practical way of having a <u>Quiet</u> <u>Time</u> where your fellowship with God will be strengthened and deepened. This is called the PRESS method...

*P*RAY for a moment, telling God that you want to learn truth from His word that can apply to your life.

*R*EAD His Word; you might start with the Gospel of John. Pick a short section (maybe 5 verses) and read it three times.
> <u>1st reading</u> --for general background
> <u>2nd reading</u> --for main idea in section
> <u>3rd reading</u> --for personal application

*E*XAMINE His Word; take a pen and paper and start your own notebook. This will help you keep track of what God teaches you. As you examine the passage of Scripture, write down insights using *S.P.A.C.E.* method:

<u>S.P.A.C.E.</u> method

<u>S</u>ins to confess.
  (Things you are doing wrong)

<u>P</u>romises to claim.
  (What God tells you He will do for us)

<u>A</u>ctions to avoid.
  (Warnings never to do certain things)

<u>C</u>ommands to obey.
  (Things God tells you to do)

<u>E</u>xamples to follow.
  (Something done by someone else, that you should also do)

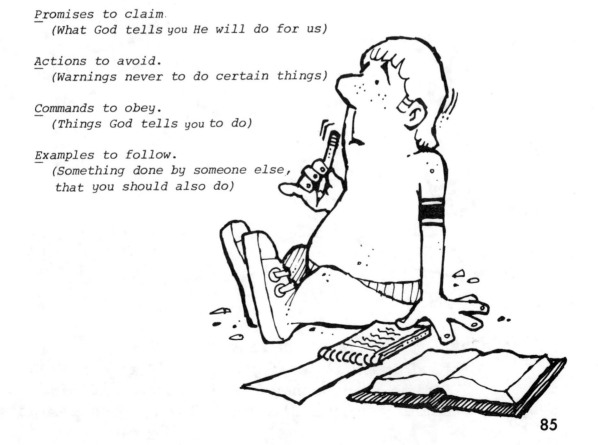

After you have done this, review your notes, asking yourself whether there are any <u>attitudes</u> in your life that God needs to change. For example, are you ungrateful? unloving? unthankful? prideful? etc.

Now think whether there is any area of your life where God desires a <u>behavior</u> change. In what areas of your life should this take place? Take a 3 x 5 card and write this area of application on it. This will help you plan your behaviour so that when you face a situation, you can respond in the way God has taught you.

S AY *back to God the things you have learned and ask Him for the power to apply His truth to your life.*

S HARE *with a Christian friend what you have found; find one with whom you can share regularly. <u>Remember</u> --you never really have anything until you give it away. Share God's insights.*

(REMOVE THIS PAGE FOR YOUR BIBLE)

Do you have a time and place that you can meet with God? Jesus met with His Father "early in the morning in a lonely place."

1. Where is a quiet place that you could meet with the Lord? _____

2. When would be a good time for you to spend talking to God and reading His Word? _____

_____

Here are practical steps for having a <u>Quiet</u> <u>Time</u>:

PRAY: Ask God to teach you truth from His Word that can apply to your life.

READ: John 5:1-18 three times
<u>1st</u> --in general
<u>2nd</u> --for main idea
<u>3rd</u> --for application

EXAMINE: Have pen and paper so that you can start your own notebook. This will help you keep track of what God teaches you. As you examine the passage of Scripture write down insights using the <u>S.P.A.C.E.</u> method

<u>S.P.A.C.E.</u> method

<u>S</u>ins to confess.
 (Things you are doing wrong)

<u>P</u>romises to claim.
 (What God tells you He will do for you)

<u>A</u>ctions to avoid.
 (Warnings not to do certain things)

<u>C</u>ommands to obey.
 (Things God tells you to do)

<u>E</u>xamples to follow.
 (Something done by someone else, that you should also do)

After you have done this, review your notes, asking yourself if there are any <u>attitudes</u> in your life that God needs to change. Are you unthankful? unloving? etc.

Now think whether there is any area of your life where God desires a <u>behavior</u> change. In what areas of your life should this take place? Take a 3 x 5 card and write these practical applications on it. This will help you plan your behavior so that when you face a situation you can respond the way God has taught you.

𝕾 AY: Back to God the things you have learned and ask Him for the power to apply His truth to your life.

𝕾 HARE: With a Christian friend what you have found; find one with whom you can share regularly. Remember, YOU NEVER REALLY HAVE ANYTHING UNTIL YOU GIVE IT AWAY.

"QUIET TIME HELPS"
RELATED TO
YOUR QUIET TIME

WHAT THE QUIET TIME HELPS ARE ALL ABOUT

Every Christian needs to get quiet before God and take time to study the Bible--and worship God through prayer and praise.

After each discussion in this manual there are three "Quiet Time helps" which are designed to help you grow as a Christian.

It should take no more than a week for you to work your way through the three Quiet Time helps per discussion. After completing the three lessons you should sit down and discuss them with the person who is assisting you with the Discussion Manual for Student Discipleship.

QUIET TIME-QUIET TIME 1,2,3

This week you will study the book of II Thessalonians. You will read one chapter at a time. There are three chapters -- so that will make three quiet times. The purpose of these quiet times is for God to speak to you through His Word, and for you to speak to Him through prayer.

STEPS

STEP ONE: As you sit down with your study sheet, Bible, and pen--take a moment to _pray_. Ask God to teach you new and encouraging truths from His Word.

STEP TWO: Read the chapter once quickly -- don't stop at any point yet.

STEP THREE: Read it again slowly -- taking time to record insights you get from the chapter. You will want to be looking for:

1. Things Paul is teaching the people in Thessalonica.
2. Insights into what problems the people there might have.
3. Things for which Paul encourages them -- what is good about their church.
4. Anything else God might show you.

Record the verse from which you draw the insight in the VERSE COLUMN.

Record a key phrase or few words from the actual Bible verse in the BIBLE TEXT COLUMN.

Record your personal insights from the verse under the PERSONAL INSIGHTS COLUMN.

STEP FOUR: When you finish the chapter, record one truth that will affect your life this week. This is one that you learned from your study. Record _how_ it will affect your life.

STEP FIVE: Take a moment and pray that God will, by His Spirit, make the above truth part of your life. You might also take time now to pray for other personal needs and friends.

QUIET TIME 1

BOOK _____ CHAPTER _____ DATE _____

CHAPTER THEME _____

_____

VERSES   BIBLE TEXT   PERSONAL INSIGHT

ONE TRUTH THAT WILL AFFECT MY LIFE THIS WEEK

QUIET TIME 2

BOOK _____ CHAPTER _____ DATE _____

CHAPTER THEME _____

_____

| VERSES | BIBLE TEXT | PERSONAL INSIGHT |

ONE TRUTH THAT WILL AFFECT MY LIFE THIS WEEK

QUIET TIME 3

BOOK _____ CHAPTER _____ DATE _____

CHAPTER THEME _____

_____

VERSES	BIBLE TEXT	PERSONAL INSIGHT

ONE TRUTH THAT WILL AFFECT MY LIFE THIS WEEK

The importance of
YOUR PRAYER
DiSCUSSiON 6

One of the most <u>important</u> (yet often difficult) arts for a Christian to learn and experience is the art of prayer.

Luke 11:1
"And it came about that while He was praying in a certain place, after He had finished, one of His disciples said to Him, "Lord, teach us to pray just as John also taught his disciples."

●Why do you think praying to God is so important?

_____

●Can you think of some reasons why prayer is so often difficult? _____

_____

●Why did the disciples ask Christ to teach them to pray? _____

_____

Right now...

- *define prayer*
- *learn why a Christian should pray*
- *look at our manner of prayer*
- *check conditions necessary for answered prayer*

WHAT IS PRAYER?

1. Prayer is coming into the presence of God.

Hebrews 4:16
"Let us therefore draw near <u>with</u> <u>confidence</u> to the throne of grace, that we may receive mercy and may find grace to help in time of need."

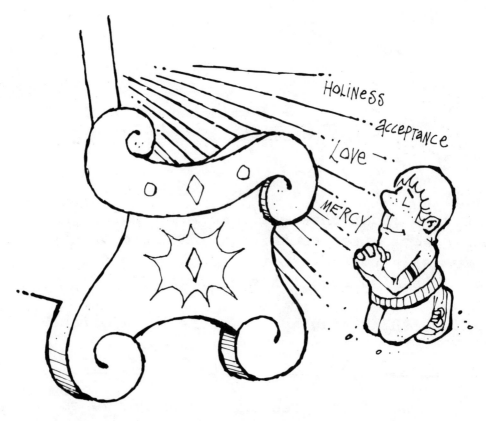

When you come into the presence of God (to this throne of grace) you can be assured that you are in close contact with Him.

According to Hebrews 4:16, what attitude should you have when meeting with God? _____

What is the "throne of grace?" _____

_____

> Grace is when God actively pours
> out His love to you, <u>not because
> you deserve it</u>, but because Christ
> died for you (which was also an
> act of grace), and because God
> deeply cares for you.

2. Prayer is communicating our love to God.

HERE IS THE MODEL FOR PRAYER THAT JESUS SHARED WITH HIS DISCIPLES:

Matthew 6:9-13 (Phillips)
"Our heavenly Father, <u>may your name be honored</u>;
May your kingdom come, and your will be done
on earth as it is in heaven. Give us this day
the <u>bread we need</u>, <u>forgive us what we owe to you</u>,
as we have also forgiven those who owe anything
to us. <u>Keep us clear of temptation</u>, and <u>save us
from evil</u>."

When Jesus prayed, how did He express His love
toward the Father? _____

_____

(He wanted His name to be holy;there is no higher
compliment to God --Isaiah 6:3. He wanted His
kingdom to come and His will to be done.)

What specific, practical, physical needs are
mentioned in this prayer? _____

What are some practical things you can ask God for?

What spiritual needs are mentioned in this prayer?

_____

(Forgiveness of sins; deliverance from temptation.)

3. Prayer is letting God communicate back to you.

Philippians 4:6-7
"Be anxious for
nothing, but in
everything by prayer
and supplication with
thanksgiving let your
requests be made known
to God. And the
peace of God, which
surpasses all
comprehension, shall
guard your hearts and
your minds in Christ
Jesus."

Not only does prayer take care of anxiety but in
prayer God answers back, disclosing more of
Himself to you.

●What response does God give to those who in faith pray to Him? _____

> Prayer is more than simply dictating selfish desires to God, using His name as a magic word for success. _It is seeking to come within the boundaries of God's will for you._ That's why it says in...

Hosea 6:3 (Living Bible)
"Oh, that we might know the Lord! Let us press on TO KNOW HIM, and HE WILL RESPOND TO US as surely as the coming of dawn or the rain of early spring."

> PRAYER THEREFORE is...
> Coming into the presence of God, confidently expressing our love and _needs_ (not "wants") to Him, and letting Him communicate back to you His leading for your life.

Here are a few benefits of prayer.

1. Prayer gives deep joy.

John 16:23-24
"...if you shall ask the Father for anything, He will give it to you in My name...ask, and you will receive, _that your joy may be made full._

As you ask God to _meet_ _your_ _needs_ and then see Him answer, this is great! Your Christian life _comes alive_ and you are thrilled to see Him do mighty things in answer to your prayers!

2. Prayer works to change lives and events in everyday life.

James 5:17-18
"Elijah was a man with a nature like ours, and he prayed earnestly that it might not rain; and it did not rain on the earth for three years and six months. And he prayed again, and the sky poured rain, and the earth produced its fruit."

Was Elijah any different than you in nature? _____

Can you think of specific things you've prayed for that God has answered? _____

_____

_____

3. Prayer increases our love for those who are seemingly hard to love.

Luke 6:27-28
"But I say to you who hear, love your enemies, do good to those who hate you, bless those who curse you, pray for those who mistreat you."

Why would praying for people cause you to love them more? _____

_____

(You begin to see their needs...As you pray, God gives you His perspective toward their needs.)

4. Prayer glorifies God.

John 14:13
"And whatever you ask in My name, that will I do, that the Father may be glorified in the Son."

Why is it so important that God gets the praise for all that's done? _____

_____

(He is eternal. He is worthy as the great Creator God.)

PRAYER THEREFORE BENEFITS YOU BY:

- giving deep joy
- working to change lives and events in everyday life
- increasing your love for those who are seemingly hard to love
- glorifying God

Some hindrances and some guidelines to prayer.

 Prayer is not making God a "cosmic bellhop," trying to get Him to do what you want. God has set down conditions and guidelines for true prayer. These guidelines are yours to make sure God's love and glory are truly seen.

Here are some guidelines for us to consider...

A. You must pray according to God's will.

I John 5:14-15
"And this is the confidence which we have before Him, that, if we ask anything according to His will, He hears us. And if we know that He hears us in whatever we ask, we know that we have the requests which we have asked from Him."

It is true that God has set up a system in which your prayer causes God to act. Yet, He will only act for you when you pray in accordance with His will for you, so far as answering your specific prayer is concerned.

John 15:7-8
"If you abide in Me, and My words abide in you, ask whatever you wish, and it shall be done for you. By this is My Father glorified, that you bear much fruit, and so prove to be My disciples."

B. You must not have unconfessed sin in your life.

Psalm 66:18
"If I regard wickedness in my heart, the Lord will not hear..."

●Why is it that God will not answer prayer when there is unconfessed sin in your life? _____

_____

_____

(Because you make a mockery of His holiness. Because it looks as though He does not really care if you sin or not. And because soon, in your rebellion, you will lose motivation to get things right with Him and with others.)

This is why James says...

James 4:3
"You ask and do not receive, because you ask with
wrong motives, so that you may spend it on your
pleasures."

C. God has the option to answer your prayers with
a _yes_, a _no_, or a _wait_ response.

> It is important that, in any
> answer to prayer you receive
> from God, you remain thankful.
> _All_ of His answers are more
> evidence of His love to you.

God sometimes says NO.

The Apostle Paul had a physical problem which
caused him great pain. He asked God three times
to do something about it. But God said, "No,"
and even gave Paul a reason.

II Corinthians 12:8-9
"Concerning this I entreated the Lord three times
that it might depart from me. And He has said to
me, 'My grace is sufficient for you, for power
is perfected in weakness.' Most gladly, therefore,
I will rather boast about my weaknesses, that the
power of Christ may dwell in me."

● Why did God refuse Paul's request? _____

_____

(Because God wanted to show Paul and others the
vastness of His grace.)

God sometimes says WAIT.

Waiting creates a _trial_ which should cause you to
grow in faith and patience toward God.

(See Chapter Three on TRIALS)

God also says YES.

Usually when you seek God, and are praying to Him according to His will, He answers your prayer over and beyond what you ever dreamed because God loves you so much.

GUIDELINES TO PRAYER...

- _pray according to God's will_

- _don't have unconfessed sin in your life_

- _be open to God as He exercises His option to answer NO, WAIT, or YES_

- _remain thankful to Him regardless of His answer, since love is His motive and He knows all things_

Let's Summarize...

What is prayer?

- it is coming into the presence of God
- it is communicating your love to God
- it is letting God communicate back to you

What are prayer's benefits?

- prayer gives deep joy
- prayer works to change lives and events in everyday life
- prayer increases your love for those who are seemingly hard to love
- prayer glorifies God

What are prayer's guidelines?

- pray according to God's will
- don't have unconfessed sin in your life
- be open to God's NO, WAIT, or YES options
- remain thankful to Him regardless of His answer to you

Since prayer is so important, and has such great effect in bringing glory to God and meeting our needs, what time tomorrow could you set aside to pray? _____ Can you make this time each day? Remember, God is much more concerned about you talking to Him, because of His great love for you, than you could ever be.

106

"QUIET TIME HELPS"
RELATED TO
YOUR PRAYER

WHAT THE QUIET TIME HELPS ARE ALL ABOUT

Every Christian needs to get quiet before God and take time to study the Bible--and worship God through prayer and praise.

After each discussion in this manual there are three "Quiet Time helps" which are designed to help you grow as a Christian.

It should take no more than a week for you to work your way through the three Quiet Time helps per discussion. After completing the three lessons you should sit down and discuss them with the person who is assisting you with the Discussion Manual for Student Discipleship.

PRAYER QUIET TIME 1

SUBJECT: <u>THE IMPORTANCE OF PRAYER</u>

What does God tell you about your prayers?

Proverbs 15:8 _____

_____

What is God's attitude toward you when you pray?

Psalm 34:18 _____

Psalm 119:151 _____

Psalm 145:18, 19 _____

_____

Deuteronomy 4:7 _____

What did Jesus teach about prayer?

Luke 5:16 _____

Luke 6:12 _____

Luke 9:18 _____

Luke 9:28 _____

Mark 11:22-25 _____

_____

Matthew 6:5-6 _____

_____

Luke 11:9-13 _____

_____

_____

_____

_____

What did Paul teach concerning prayer?

Colossians 4:2 _____

Ephesians 6:18 _____

_____

What was significant about Epaphras?

Colossians 4:12 _____

Would you say prayer is always easy? _____ *Why?* _____

_____

_____

_____

God wants you to pray, He is near to listen, and wants to answer.
What should you pray about?

Philippians 4:6-7 _____

_____

I Peter 5:6-7 _____

_____

This week pray three times for 1/2 hour. During this time tell God your concerns
your problems, your frustrations, your short comings. Ask Him to help you and
others. Then take some time to listen to Him. Sit silently for a while and allo
Him to speak to you. When will you spend these 1/2 hour times? Record the time
below:

day _____ time _____

day _____ time _____

day _____ time _____

PRAYER QUIET TIME 2

SUBJECT: <u>THE IMPORTANCE OF LISTENING TO GOD IN PRAYER</u>

Read Ecclesiastes 5:1

What does Solomon say to do at the house of God? _____

Why do you think this is important? _____

_____

_____

_____

_____

Read Numbers 9:8

When Moses was faced with a hard decision, what did he do? _____

_____

_____

Read Deuteronomy 1:41-43

Why did the Lord not want Israel to fight? _____

_____

What had they done wrong? _____

_____

Read Mark 9:7

What was God's command concerning your relationship to Jesus? _____

_____

_____

All these passages have one thing in common -- they all tell you of the importance of _____ to God.

Often you think of prayer only in terms of God listening to you, but you must recognize that true prayer involves listening to Him, as well as His listening to you.

Read Habakkuk 2:1

What should be your attitude as you listen? _____

_____

From the following verses, record what will happen if you listen?

Psalm 85:8 _____

_____

_____

Psalm 34:18 _____

_____

_____

Psalm 143:8-9 _____

_____

_____

God speaks to you primarily through the Bible. But He also speaks to you by bringing thoughts into your mind. You must remember that the thoughts He will bring to mind or the words He would speak will always be consistent with His Word. The point that you should realize is that you do not take very much time to listen to Him. Your prayer is usually only a list of your requests and then leaving. Take time to allow God to speak peace to you at the end of your requests.

As you pray over certain things, record any thoughts God might bring to mind during your 1/2 hour time with Him.

_____

_____

_____

_____

PRAYER QUIET TIME 3

SUBJECT: *GOD SPEAKING TO US*

In Quiet Time II the importance of listening to God was discussed. You will study Psalm 19 today and learn how God reveals Himself to people.

Read Psalm 19

As you read the Psalm, what two ways do you see that God has revealed Himself to humanity?

1. _____

2. _____

Some have said that it is impossible to know anything about God apart from the Bible--What can be known from the celestial bodies? Who can know it? (Study verses 1-6)

_____

_____

_____

_____

_____

The words in verses 7 through 10 such as law, testimony, precepts, judgments and so forth are used synonymously. List below what they can do for you.

_____

_____

_____

_____

_____

_____

_____

_____

_____

Now rewrite in your own words verses 11 through 14 from Psalm 19 as your prayer to God. When done, repeat it aloud to Him as your prayer.

_____

_____

_____

_____

_____

_____

_____

_____

_____

_____

_____

_____

The importance of
THE SPIRIT-FILLED LIFE
Discussion 7

Since becoming a Christian, what kind of problems have you had in obeying God and pleasing Him?

_____

_____

_____

The biggest problem most Christians face is that they often find themselves doing the things they <u>know</u> are wrong, and <u>fail</u> to do the things they know are right. In other words, they don't do what pleases God. This leads to frustration.

Have you experienced frustration in your new life?

_____

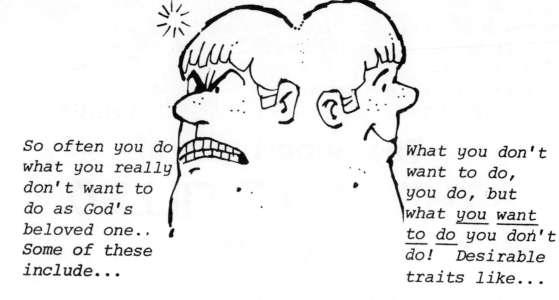

So often you do what you really don't want to do as God's beloved one.. Some of these include...

What you don't want to do, you do, but what <u>you</u> <u>want</u> <u>to</u> <u>do</u> you don't do! Desirable traits like...

(Desires of the <u>flesh</u>)

- jealousy
- lack of love for God
- lack of love for others
- guilt
- worry
- disobedience
- impure thoughts
- frustration
- critical spirit
- laziness
- overeating

(Desires of the <u>Spirit</u>)

- joy
- peace
- patience
- kindness
- goodness
- gentleness
- self-control
- faithfulness
- love

IT IS ALMOST AS THOUGH YOU HAVE A SPLIT PERSONALITY... YOU ARE AT WAR INSIDE. YOU HAVE A NATURE THAT LOVES TO REBEL, YET YOU NOW HAVE A NEW NATURE THAT WANTS TO OBEY GOD. A CONFLICT RESULTS!

But it's good to know that <u>God has the answer</u> <u>and the power to solve this nagging dilemma!</u>

116

The Bible says that the key to solving this
problem is for you to be filled with the Holy
Spirit, and walk in His power. Many Christians
don't understand, or misunderstand, this and
are powerless as a result. <u>This is unnecessary</u>.

If the key to living for Christ is in the work of
the Holy Spirit, then:
- Who is He?
  - Why did He come?
  - How does He affect me?

1. O.K., first, <u>Who is the Holy Spirit</u>?

Who do you think the Holy Spirit is? _____

_____

> The Holy Spirit is a Person. He is not a
> vapor, a phantom, or a "divine influence."

A. We know that the Holy Spirit is a Person
because Jesus Christ calls Him "He."

John 16:8
"And He, when He comes, will convict the world
concerning sin, and righteousness, and judgment."

Do you think that Jesus Christ would call the
Holy Spirit "He" if the Holy Spirit were not
a Person? _____

B. He is God. One reason we know this is
because the Bible clearly teaches that
the Holy Spirit knows everything, and <u>only
God knows everything</u>!

I Corinthians 2:10-11
"For to us God revealed them through the Spirit;
for the Spirit searches all things, even the
depths of God. For who among men knows the
thoughts of a man except the spirit of the man,
which is in him? Even so the thoughts of God
no one knows except the Spirit of God."

THE HOLY SPIRIT IS EVERYWHERE.

Psalm 139:7-10
"Where can I go from Thy Spirit? Or where can
I flee from Thy presence? If I ascend to heaven,
Thou art there; if I make my bed in Sheol (Hell),
behold, Thou art there. If I take the wings of
the dawn, if I dwell in the remotest part of the
sea, even there Thy hand will lead me, and Thy
right hand will lay hold of me."

THE HOLY SPIRIT IS ALL POWERFUL.
Zechariah 4:6
"Then he answered and said to me, 'This is the
word of the Lord to Zerubbabel saying, "Not by
might nor by power, but by my Spirit," says the
Lord of hosts.'"

THE HOLY SPIRIT IS UNSEARCHABLY GREAT.
Isaiah 40:13
"Who has directed the Spirit of the Lord, or as
His counselor has informed Him?"

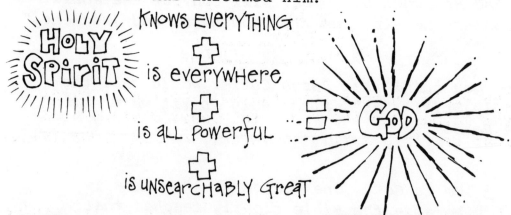

These characteristics of the Holy Spirit all add
up to Him being GOD!

118

C. He is the Third Person of the Trinity, another concept that is clearly taught in the Bible.

Matthew 28:19
"Go therefore and make disciples of all the nations, baptizing them in the name of the Father and the Son and the Holy Spirit..."

When Christ mentions the Holy Spirit, does He put the Holy Spirit on a different level than the Father or the Son? _____

The Bible teaches that the Holy Spirit is equal to the Father and the Son. Yet Jesus clearly says that the Holy Spirit is another Person (John 16:14).

D. Even though this is a mystery to you as a finite (limited) person, you know that the Holy Spirit is God and yet He is not the Father or the Son

(Jesus Christ).   But you also know that the Father, Son, and Holy Spirit work so close together that they form one thought --<u>one Person which equals God</u>.

> The Father, Son, and the Holy Spirit work so closely together that the Bible teaches that all three work in you, and yet are One Person.

<u>The Bible teaches that God is in you.</u>

I Corinthians 3:16
"Do you not know that you are a temple of God, and that the Spirit of God dwells in you?"

Your body is the temple of whom? _____

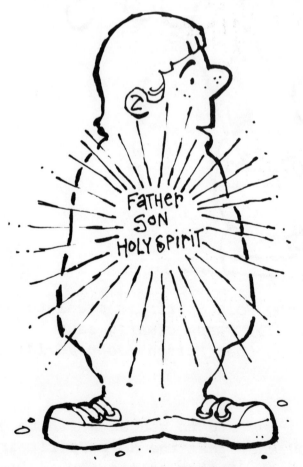

<u>The Bible teaches that Jesus Christ is in you.</u>

Colossians 1:27
"...to whom God willed to make known what is the riches of the glory of this mystery among the Gentiles, which is Christ in you, the hope of glory."

<u>The Bible teaches clearly that the Holy Spirit lives in you.</u>

I Corinthians 6:19
"Or do you not know that your body is a temple of the Holy Spirit who is in you, whom you have from God, and that you are not your own?"

Your body is the temple of whom? _____

While the Trinity is a mystery, and no diagram is adequate to explain the equality of the Father/Son/ Holy Spirit being one Person (but with different functions), this diagram may be helpful...

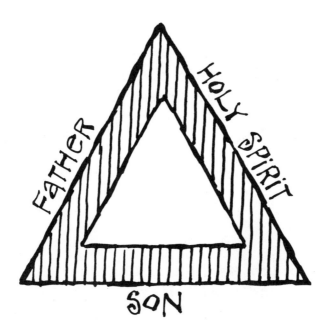

Just as the sides of a triangle are equal with each other, and make a triangle when put together, so the Father/Son/Holy Spirit are equal and together make up the Person of God. The left side of the triangle is equal to --yet not the same as-- the right side or bottom of the triangle. In the same manner the Father is equal to --yet not the same as-- the Son or the Holy Spirit. This is truly a great mystery.

2. The Holy Spirit came to bring glory to Jesus Christ the Son.

A. The Holy Spirit came to indwell the person who believes in Jesus Christ as Saviour.

Romans 8:9
"However you are not in the flesh but in the Spirit, if indeed the Spirit of God dwells in you. But if anyone does not have the Spirit of Christ, he does not belong to Him."

B. The Holy Spirit came to lead men to the truth.

John 16:13
"But when He, the Spirit of truth, comes, He will guide you into all the truth..."

C. The Holy Spirit came to bring glory to Jesus Christ the Son.

John 16:14
"He shall glorify Me (Jesus Christ); for He shall take of Mine, and shall disclose it to you."

D. The Holy Spirit came to give men the power to tell others of Jesus Christ.

Acts 1:8
"...but you shall receive power when the Holy Spirit has come upon you; and you shall be My witnesses both in Jerusalem, and in all Judea and Samaria, and even to the remotest part of the earth."

What will you be able to do after you have the power of the Holy Spirit? _____

> *Since there is an intense spiritual battle between God and the powers of darkness, a battle being fought over the lives and minds of men, you very desperately need to be empowered by the Holy Spirit!*

E. The Holy Spirit came <u>to help</u> you to live your life in a Christ-like manner.

Galations 5:22-23
"But the fruit of the Spirit is love, joy, peace, patience, kindness, goodness, faithfulness, gentleness, self-control; against such things there is no law."

THERE FORE... *For you to grow and learn more truth from God, to have power to lead others to Christ, and to live a life of victory, as Jesus Christ did, you need to be filled with the Holy Spirit.*

You now see that when you are filled with the Holy Spirit you are filled with Christ. To be filled with the Holy Spirit is to be controlled by Him in all areas of your life.

3. How can you be filled by the Holy Spirit so that you can have the power to live for God?

* You need to realize that the Bible commands you to be filled by the Holy Spirit.

Ephesians 5:18
"And do not get drunk with wine, for that is dissipation, but be filled with the Spirit..."

Would God command you to do something if it were impossible for it to happen?_____

✳ It is important that you confess your sin to God so you can be filled with His Spirit.

I John 1:9
"If we confess our sins, He is faithful and righteous to forgive us our sins and to cleanse us from all unrighteousness."

The Holy Spirit is not a "bully," so He will only control you when you let Him. Don't expect to be filled with the Holy Spirit if there is sin in your life.

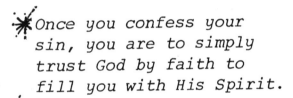

✳ Once you confess your sin, you are to simply trust God by faith to fill you with His Spirit.

Colossians 2:6
(Phillips)
"Just as you received Christ Jesus the Lord, so go on living in Him in simple faith."

You should not expect lightning or thunder when God fills you with His Spirit. <u>You will be aware of a new ability to overcome sin, and to live a life of victory as a Christian,</u> when you are filled with the Spirit.

> *Right now would be a good time for you to thank God for His Spirit, and His presence in your life. If there are sins that you have not confessed, confess them as you pray now, and ask God to fill you with His Spirit. Then, by faith, begin to live your life as a Spirit-filled believer, as one who remains sensitive to God. And you can watch and see how God's strength will enable you to live victoriously.*

"QUIET TIME HELPS" RELATED TO THE SPIRIT-FILLED LIFE

WHAT THE QUIET TIME HELPS ARE ALL ABOUT

Every Christian needs to get quiet before God and take time to study the Bible--and worship God through prayer and praise.

After each discussion in this manual there are three "Quiet Time helps" which are designed to help you grow as a Christian.

It should take no more than a week for you to work your way through the three Quiet Time helps per discussion. After completing the three lessons you should sit down and discuss them with the person who is assisting you with the Discussion Manual for Student Discipleship.

SPIRIT-FILLED LIFE QUIET TIME 1,2,3

The following passages are Jesus' own teaching on the role of the Holy Spirit. These are some of the important things He told His disciples just before He was arrested and crucified. He knew that these men would need comfort and encouragement. You should also realize that a man's last words carry a deeper significance because they are often of greater importance.

Use the system of study that you used on the Quiet Times of Chapter 5. You might remember that you studied II Thessalonians.

Remember to make personal application, step four, Chapter 5.

QUIET TIME 1 *John 14:14-21*

BOOK _____ PASSAGE _____ DATE _____

PASSAGE THEME _____

_____

VERSES	BIBLE TEXT	PERSONAL INSIGHT

ONE TRUTH THAT WILL AFFECT MY LIFE THIS WEEK

QUIET TIME 2 *John 14:25-27, 15:26-27*

BOOK _____ PASSAGE _____ DATE _____

PASSAGE THEME _____

_____

VERSES	BIBLE TEXT	PERSONAL INSIGHT

ONE TRUTH THAT WILL AFFECT MY LIFE THIS WEEK

QUIET TIME 3 *John 16:7-16*

BOOK _____ PASSAGE _____ DATE _____

PASSAGE THEME _____

_____

VERSES	BIBLE TEXT	PERSONAL INSIGHT

ONE TRUTH THAT WILL AFFECT MY LIFE THIS WEEK

The importance of
WALKING IN THE SPIRIT

Discussion 8

●*Did you know that God wants you to walk with Him moment-by-moment in every detail of your life?*

GOD'S CONCERN FOR EVERY DETAIL...

Psalm 37:23
"The steps of a man are established by the Lord; and He delights in his way."

Can you name some steps (things you do in your daily life schedule) that you take each day? _____

_____

Does God become bored with the details of your daily life and your activities? _____

PROOF OF GOD'S CONCERN FOR YOU...

Psalm 139:17-18
"How precious also are Thy thoughts to me, O God!
How vast is the sum of them! If I should count them
they would outnumber the sand. When I awake, I am
still with Thee."

Is God passive or active in His thoughts about you?

_____

According to the above verses, how many precious
thoughts does God have toward you? _____

YOUR RESPONSE TO GOD'S CONCERN...

Colossians 2:6
"As you therefore have received Christ Jesus the
Lord, so walk in Him."

* When you received Christ, it was by simple faith
* By simple trust, you have a moment-by-moment walk
   that is full of adventure, meaning and growth.

> If you are filled with the Holy Spirit (that's
> trusting God and doing what He wants you to do),
> every minute of life can be one fantastic and
> meaningful adventure!

LET'S GET INTO...

...how a Christian can mess up the walk that God so
desires to have with him. But then let's see how
to _practically_ walk with God minute by minute.

MESSING UP OUR WALK...

You can disrupt your intimate walk with God by just
breaking one of His basic commands for your life.

134

Ephesians 4:30
"And <u>do</u> <u>not</u> <u>grieve</u> the Holy Spirit of God, by whom
you were sealed for the day of redemption.

●What is it to <u>grieve</u> someone?_____

 (To deeply hurt them.)

●God never forces us to do anything. He only wants
 us to respond to Him by turning from the wrong we
 do. <u>Because of this, we are given the ingredients</u>
 <u>for grieving the Holy Spirit Who dwells within us.</u>
 (This is possible because we have free choice.)

●It is very easy to grieve
 because He is absolutely
 Holy, and we aren't.

 I John 1:5
 "And this is the message we
 have heard from Him and
 announce to you, that God
 is light, and in
 Him there is no
 darkness at all."

HOW YOU CAN GRIEVE THE HOLY SPIRIT...

The Apostle Paul mentions many things that grieve
the Holy Spirit, when he writes in Ephesians 4 & 5.

 ●lying (Ephesians 4:25)
 ●anger (Ephesians 4:26)
 ●theft (Ephesians 4:28)
 ●evil speaking, impure thoughts and actions, foolish-
  ness, unseemly jesting (Ephesians 4:25; 5:3-4)
 ●bitterness, wrath, spite (Ephesians 4:31)
 ●fornication, greed (Ephesians 5:3)

135

✳ *The Holy Spirit, being the Spirit of <u>Holiness</u>, (Romans 1:4), is grieved by all impurity, filthiness, and any contact with evil.*

✳ *Since the Holy Spirit is the Spirit of <u>wisdom</u>, <u>understanding</u>, and <u>knowledge</u> (Isaiah 11:2), then:*

   "Remaining in ignorance of spiritual truths, no zeal in Bible study, grieves Him."

✳ *Since the Holy Spirit is the Spirit of <u>faith</u> (II Corinthians 4:13), then your doubts, discouragements, anxieties, constant worrying, etc., grieves Him.*

WHAT'S HAPPENING?

A. *When you grieve Him, He does not leave you, shrink way, or stop loving you, but <u>remains</u> with you always.*

   John 14:16
   "And I will ask the Father, and He will give you another Helper, that He may be with you forever..."

B. *When you grieve Him, you <u>lose both your power</u> and <u>your joy</u>, plus your fellowship with God.*

   Psalm 32:3-4 (David's words, after his great sin)
   "When I kept silent about my sin, my body wasted away through my groaning all day long. For day and night Thy hand was heavy upon me; my vitality was drained away as with the fever heat of summer."

C. *When you grieve Him, His work in your life changes from one of power to one of <u>pleading</u> for you to yield to Him.*

D. *When you are <u>sorrowful</u> over sin you've committed, it is often the Holy Spirit helping you to realize how deeply you've hurt God by not trusting Him.*

MOMENT-BY-MOMENT WALK.

Since you now know how to mess up your walk by grieving the Holy Spirit, let's take a look at how you can walk moment-by-moment in the Spirit.

● *Walking in the Spirit can be very practical...*

1.

Here you come, down the hall at school, when who do you see approaching but Bill B. Basketball, #1 star player of the school team. You are green with envy, wishing you could be as popular as Bill.

2.

You have just grieved the Holy Spirit. Instead of letting the Holy Spirit love through you, you followed the inclinations of your sin nature and became jealous and envious.

3.

Consequently, you have lost the power to live the truly victorious Christian life, and you are now open to all kinds of sins (lust, worry, impure thoughts, etc.).

4.

Suddenly the Holy Spirit, through your memory of the Word of God, convicts you of the sin you have just committed. You realize you must do something about your sin. So...

5.

As you continue to walk down the hall, you confess your sin, agreeing with God that you were wrong.

6.

Now that your sin is confessed, you know it is God's command to be filled with the Spirit. So you, by faith, accept the fact that you are filled with the Holy Spirit.

7.

Now you thank God that you are filled with the Holy Spirit.

8.

You walk on to class empowered by the Holy Spirit, in fellowship with God, and ready to share your new life in Christ.

WRAPPING IT ALL UP...

Since you have learned how important your moment-by-moment walk with God is, you should also bear in mind how easy it is to grieve the Holy Spirit.

• Will you begin to walk in the Spirit --quickly confessing your sins and allowing God to fill you with His power and joy? _____

> As you learn to walk in the Spirit, your fellowship with God will grow deeper and deeper, allowing you to learn more about the great love God has for you.

"QUIET TIME HELPS" RELATED TO WALKING IN THE SPIRIT

WHAT THE QUIET TIME HELPS ARE ALL ABOUT

Every Christian needs to get quiet before God and take time to study the Bible--and worship God through prayer and praise.

After each discussion in this manual there are three "Quiet Time helps" which are designed to help you grow as a Christian.

It should take no more than a week for you to work your way through the three Quiet Time helps per discussion. After completing the three lessons you should sit down and discuss them with the person who is assisting you with the Discussion Manual for Student Discipleship.

WALK IN THE SPIRIT QUIET TIME 1

SUBJECT: THE SELF-CENTERED FLESHLY WALK VS. THE SPIRIT-FILLED WALK

Read Galatians 5:13-26

How is walking in the Spirit described?

vs. 13 _____

_____

What are the results of the self-centered fleshly walk?

vs. 15 _____

_____

What is the key to overcoming the flesh?

v. 16, v. 25 _____

Describe the battle between the flesh and the Spirit.

v. 17 _____

_____

List the qualities of the flesh-centered life and the Spirit-filled life.

Flesh-centered, v. 19-21 _____

_____

_____

Spirit-filled, v. 22-23 _____

_____

_____

What is the condition of your flesh if you know Christ?

vs. 24 _____

Why is it difficult to practically believe this?

_____

List the three opposite characteristics of the Spirit-filled life and what they mean - v. 26.

Characteristic _____

What it means _____

Characteristic _____

What it means _____

Characteristic _____

What it means _____

The key to the Spirit-filled walk is to "live by the Spirit" and "walk by the Spirit". What does this practically mean? Record your thoughts.

_____

_____

_____

WaLK IN THE SPIRIT QUIET TIME 2

Read I Thessalonians 2:1-12

Carefully examine this passage and list the characteristics of Paul as he walked in the Holy Spirit. Remember the walk in the Spirit will reflect: love, joy, peace, patience, kindness, goodness, gentleness, faithfulness, self-control.

WRITE OUT THE TEXT OF THE VERSE	RECORD CHARACTERISTIC

Which fruit of the Spirit have you lacked recently?

_____

Briefly explain why you've had difficulty in this area.

_____

_____

_____

_____

As you spend time in prayer, ask God to take your weakness and turn it into His strength.

WALK IN THE SPIRIT QUIET TIME 3

How would you describe the walk in the Spirit? Record your description before doing this study:

_____

_____

_____

_____

What do the following verses tell you about your walk as a Christian?

Romans 8:4 _____

_____

_____

II Corinthians 5:7 _____

_____

_____

Acts 1:8 _____

_____

_____

I John 2:6 _____

_____

_____

Ephesians 5:2 _____

_____

_____

The following verses show some of Jesus' thoughts concerning the walk in the Spirit. How does He describe it?

Matthew 5:23-24 _____

_____

_____

Matthew 5:41 _____

_____

_____

Matthew 20:25-28 _____

_____

_____

Luke 6:35-38 _____

_____

_____

Luke 12:15 _____

_____

_____

In light of what you have just studied, rewrite your description of the walk in the Spirit. Does it differ from your first description?

_____

_____

_____

_____

The importance of
YOUR FELLOWSHIP
Discussion 9

THE BODY

One of the most exciting things about becoming a
Christian is that you now have joined a "family."
Your new family includes <u>all</u> those who believe in
Jesus Christ. God calls all these people who
trust Christ, "The Body of Christ".

BROTHERS AND SISTERS

God uses these members ("brothers and sisters")
of His family to affect your walk with Him. They
help and contribute to you <u>greatly</u>. The members
in the family are to

- listen to you
- share with you
- encourage you
- love you with Christian love
- help you grow in your knowledge of Jesus

> It is, therefore, important for you to spend
> time getting to know other Christians...
> In fact, _God wants you to do this!_

I Corinthians 12:25
"...that there should be no division in the _body_
(fellow Christians), but that the members (those
people who believe in Christ, like you do) should
have the _same_ _care_ _for_ _one_ _another_."

What attitude should you have and show to those
who, like you, love Jesus Christ? _____

Can you think of someone this last week (a Christian)
whom you cared for or who cared for you? _____

_____

> Often the truth about fellowship with other
> Christians is overlooked or ignored. Yet a
> _very important part of your Christian life_
> _is your fellowship!_

So LET'S GET DEEPER INTO THIS.

You need to see why coming together and sharing in
the lives of other Christians is so important, and
just how it will help you grow.

1. Fellowship is close giving and sharing with
   other Christians. The _first_ _reason_ for this
   fellowship is because there is so much going
   on around you that isn't according to God's
   plan at all. (This includes our non-Christian
   friends.) _God wants you to be careful about_
   who you turn to for advice.

Psalm 1:1-2
"How blessed is the man who _does not walk in the_
counsel of the wicked, nor stand in the path of

sinners, <u>nor sit in the seat of scoffers</u>. But
his delight is in the law of the Lord, and in His
law he meditates day and night."

God says you will be happy (blessed) if you refrain
from doing what three things? _____

_____

_____

(Walking in the counsel of the wicked, standing in
the path of sinners, sitting in the seat of scoffers.)

What does <u>counsel</u> mean? _____

(Taking advice from someone.)

What does <u>stand in the path of sinners</u> mean? _____

_____

(Going along with what sinners do.)

What does <u>sit in the seat of scoffers</u> mean? _____

_____

_____

(A person will usually hang around --<u>sit</u>-- with the
people who influence him; plus, a scornful, scoffing
person tends to <u>sit</u> and criticize others, rather than
<u>doing</u> anything himself.)

> God wants you to make sure that you are drawing
> your closest friendships from those who have a
> heart for God.

I Corinthinas 15:33
"Do not be deceived: 'bad company corrupts good
morals'."

151

*How does this undesirable counsel hamper
your love for Christ?*

2. *The second reason for Christian fellowship is
in order for you to encourage your brothers
and sisters to live for Christ.*

Hebrews 10:24-25
*"...and let us consider how to stimulate one
another to love and good deeds, not forsaking our
own assembling together, as is the habit of some,
but encouraging one another; and all the more, as
you see the day drawing near."*

●*What does it mean to stimulate one another to love
and good deeds?* _____

_____

*(Getting one another "charged" and helping each
other do things pleasing to God.)*

●What does it mean by not forsaking your own
assembling together? _____

_____

(Not becoming a "freelance" Christian who thinks
he doesn't need the Body of Christ.)

●What mistake are people making when they say,
"I don't need to meet with other Christians;
they can worship alone?" _____

_____

(Whether you know it or not, you <u>need</u> the love and
the insights of other Christians.)

●As you see your world nearing what may be the climax
of history, why is it even more important that you
come together? _____

_____

(As things get worse, you will need others more,
both for encouragement and effectiveness.)

Why is what is taking place in this illustration
so much better than what is happening in the first
diagram?

3. Thirdly, God wants you to come together with other Christians so that if you fall, your good Christian friends will help you.

Ecclesiastes 4:9-12
"Two are better than one because they have a good return for their labor. For if either of them falls, the one will lift up his companion. But woe to the one who falls when there is not another to lift him up. Furthermore, if two lie down together they keep warm, but how can one be warm alone? And if one can overpower him who is alone, two can resist him. A cord of three strands is not quickly torn apart."
easily broken."

Why are two people (Christians living for God) better than one? _____

(They can accomplish more, with better results.)

What does God want you to do when you have trouble in your life? _____

_____

II Timothy 2:22
"Now flee from youthful lusts, and pursue righteousness, faith, love and peace, <u>with those who call on the Lord from a pure heart.</u>"

Are you supposed to try and get out of your problems and hang-ups all alone? _____

(You are encouraged to seek help from brothers and sisters, and this help stems from fellowship.)

4. <u>Fourthly</u>, God wants you to show a lonely, lost world your love for your brothers and sisters in Christ.

154

John 13:34-35
"A new commandment I give to you, that you love one another, even as I have loved you, that you also love one another. By this all men will know that you are My disciples, if you have love for one another."

How much did Jesus love you? _____
(Enough to die for you and to give you abundant life.)

Did Christ just die for the socially-pleasing people?

How will men know that you are really His disciple?

Did you know that God is not pleased when you ignore fellow Christians who may not be quite your type of people --personality-wise, age-wise, or otherwise?

Romans 15:1-2

"Now we who are strong ought to bear the weaknesses of those without strength and not just please ourselves. Let each of us please his neighbor for his good, to his edification."

To whom do you have responsibility? _____

_____

(To God and to each other.)

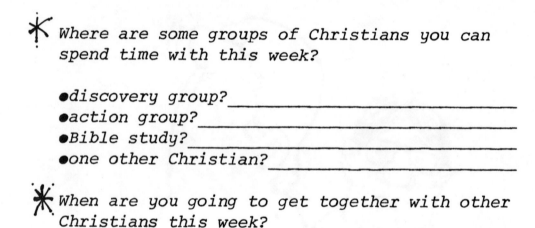

It is relatively easy for people who have never met Christ to show some human concern for those who are like them. But the real mark of your true Christianity is when you meet the needs of, and share with, other people --EVEN IF THEY ARE NOT SOCIALLY WITH-IT.

✳ *Where are some groups of Christians you can spend time with this week?*

●*discovery group?* _____
●*action group?* _____
●*Bible study?* _____
●*one other Christian?* _____

✳ *When are you going to get together with other Christians this week?* _____

"QUIET TIME HELPS" RELATED TO YOUR FELLOWSHIP

WHAT THE QUIET TIME HELPS ARE ALL ABOUT

Every Christian needs to get quiet before God and take time to study the Bible--and worship God through prayer and praise.

After each discussion in this manual there are three "Quiet Time helps" which are designed to help you grow as a Christian.

It should take no more than a week for you to work your way through the three Quiet Time helps per discussion. After completing the three lessons you should sit down and discuss them with the person who is assisting you with the Discussion Manual for Student Discipleship.

FELLOWSHIP QUIET TIME 51

SUBJECT: GOD CREATES A NEW COMMUNITY

The book of Acts tells of the beginning of the church.   God formed
a group of caring, loving, sharing people from a group of frightened,
selfish, confused individuals.   In this study, you shall look at their
relationships with each other and see what God's community of people
should be like.

What was the foundation of this community?

Acts 2:38-41 _____

_____

_____

The new community was based upon a very important relationship that
each individual had.   What was that relationship and with whom did
they have it?

I Corinthians 1:9 _____

_____

What four things were those people continually devoting themselves to?
What do they mean?   Acts 2:42

What they were devoted to   What it means

1.   1.

2.   2.

3.   3.

4.   4.

What were the results of their devotion?

Acts 2:43-47 _____

_____

159

Which two of these things do you find most present in your fellow-shipping with other Christians?

_____

Which two are most lacking?

_____

From the study you have just done, list a couple ways you could improve the new community that you're a part of:

_____

_____

FELLOWSHIP QUIET TIME 2

The Bible records some very good reasons for you to have continual close friendship and fellowship with Christians.

List some reasons from the following verses:

Proverbs 13:20 _____

Proverbs 27:17 _____

Psalm 133:1 _____

Hebrews 10:24 _____

The Bible also records a super-friendship between David and Jonathan.

From I Samuel 20:42, on what person did David and Jonathan base their relationship?

_____

What was Jonathan's attitude toward David?

I Samuel 20:17 _____

This is the type of relationship you can and should have with other members of God's family.

Let's look at this friendship in practical action. Read I Samuel 23:15-18. Saul was king of Israel and Jonathan's father. David had won a number of military victories which made him famous in Israel. King Saul became jealous of David and was trying to kill him. Jonathan knew that David was very discouraged and afraid.

What did Jonathan do to help David? _____

_____

How did he encourage David? _____

_____

Who has been a Jonathan in your life recently, encouraging you when you needed it?

_____

How did they help you? _____

_____

What qualification does John give if you are to have the best possible friendships? What does this mean?

I John 1:7 _____

_____

_____

What two things does Paul tell you that you should be involved in doing for one another?

Galatians 6:2 _____

Galatians 6:10 _____

List four ways this could practically occur:

1. _____   _____

2. _____   _____

3. _____   _____

4. _____   _____

In the blank to the right of the above statements, put the name of your friends that could use that specific encouragement.

Spend time in prayer for each of these people and ask God to build these relationships that they might be strong and honoring to Him.

FELLOWSHIP QUIET TIME 3

SUBJECT: "ONE ANOTHER" STUDY

One of the most important elements of life is learning how to relate with other people. The Bible teaches many things that deal with this subject. The following verses tell how you should get along with fellow Christians. You will notice all these verses contain the words "one another". List insights concerning how you should relate to one another from the following verses:

John 13:34-35 _____

_____

Romans 12:16 _____

_____

Romans 13:8 _____

_____

Romans 14:13 _____

_____

Romans 14:19 _____

_____

Romans 15:7 _____

_____

Romans 15:14 _____

_____

Galatians 5:13 _____

_____

Galatians 5:26 _____

_____

Galatians 6:2 _____

_____

Ephesians 4:2 _____

_____

Ephesians 4:25 _____

_____

Ephesians 4:32 _____

_____

Colossians 3:9 _____

_____

Colossians 3:13 _____

_____

Hebrews 10:24 _____

_____

James 4:11 _____

_____

James 5:16 _____

_____

I Peter 4:9 _____

_____

I Peter 5:5 _____

_____

I John 1:7 _____

_____

From all these verses, pick two that really communicated to you. List the specific ways that they tell you to relate to another person, then write out how you will actually do this in the coming days.

Verse	What it tells us to do	How I will apply it
Romans 14:13	*"let us not judge one another"*	*I am tempted to believe what a friend told me about a new Christian, Bill. But tomorrow I'll talk with him at lunch and find out the truth, I will not judge him on "hear say".*

The importance of
SHARING YOUR FAITH
Discussion 10

AN EXCITING EVENT!

A very exciting and fulfilling event occurs when you, as a new Christian, have an opportunity to share your faith in Jesus Christ.

THINK BACK FOR 2 MOMENT...

What would you consider the greatest discovery of your life?

_____

How did you hear about Jesus Christ?

_____

_____

What do you think would be the best thing you could do for the people around you?

_____

_____

Isn't it great to know that someone cared about you enough to share God's wonderful gift of the Lord Jesus Christ?

Consider the importance of sharing your faith. Look at questions like...

● Does God desire that you share Jesus Christ?

● What do you share when you "witness" to others; what is your message?

● What are some things you should know about <u>how to</u> share your faith in the Lord Jesus Christ?

WHAT DOES GOD WANT YOU TO DO?

Jesus said to those who believe in Him, follow Him, and in whom He lives:

Mark 16:15
"Go into all the world and preach the gospel to all creation."

1. Are you a follower of Jesus Christ? _____

2. What did Jesus tell you to do? _____

_____

3. What are you to proclaim? _____

> **GOSPEL =**
> ...the good news about Jesus Christ and what He did regarding sin

Matthew 28:19-20
"Go therefore and make disciples of all the nations, baptizing them in the name of the Father and the Son and the Holy Spirit, teaching them to observe all that I commanded you; and lo, I am with you always, even to the end of the age."

•What does Jesus command those who follow Him to do?

_____

You need to realize that Jesus calls not only His disciples, preachers and missionaries to proclaim the good news about Him, but He calls you to share also.

WHAT DOES GOD WANT YOUR MESSAGE TO BE?

(to those who do not know Christ personally)

You have seen in Mark 16:15 that you are to proclaim the "gospel" to all creation. The word "gospel" means "good news." Let's look into this deeper...

I Corinthians 15:1a, 3, 4
"Now I make known unto you, brethren, <u>the gospel</u>, which I preached to you... For I delivered to you as of first importance what I also received, that <u>Christ died for our sins</u> according to the Scriptures, and that <u>He was buried</u>, and that <u>He was raised on the third day</u> according to the Scriptures..."

● Who is the <u>Central Person</u> of the gospel? _____

_____

● What are the <u>three basic elements</u> of the gospel?

_____

_____

170

THE APOSTLE PETER SAID...

Acts 4:12
"And there is _salvation_ in no one else; for there is
no other name (other than Jesus Christ) under heaven
that has been given among men, by which we must be
saved."

•What is not to be found in anyone but Jesus Christ?

_____

John 3:16
"For God so loved the world, that He gave His only
begotten Son, that whosoever believes in Him should
not perish, but have eternal life."

•What motivated God to give His Son? _____

•What happens to those who _believe_ in Jesus Christ?

GOD'S LOVE FOR YOU & YOUR FRIENDS

You see that the gospel centers around the person
of Jesus Christ and His love for mankind. He,
alone, offers salvation to a lost world. You see
that He died for our sins, was buried, and now
lives to offer salvation to all who would _believe_
in Him.

•OTHER VERSES: John 14:6; Romans 10:9-10;
                 II Corinthians 5:18-120

Now that you understand God's desire for you to share
Jesus Christ, and you know basically what to share
about Him...

WHAT DOES GOD WANT YOU TO KNOW ABOUT WITNESSING?

A. You must be _in fellowship with Jesus Christ_ to be an effective witness.

John 15:5
"I am the vine, you are the branches; He who _abides in Me_, and I in him, he bears much fruit; for apart from Me you can do _nothing_."

●What is the key to bearing fruit?_____

_____

(Abiding in Christ = living in a continual, exciting relationship with Him)

●What does it mean to bear fruit?_____

_____

_____

(Bearing fruit is the evidence of God's working in your life. It can be attitude changes -- becoming loving and joyful -- or it can be the lives of all those people you lead to Jesus Christ.)

●What fruit can you bear apart from Jesus Christ?

_____

B. You must be filled with the power of the Holy Spirit to be an effective witness. (See the Discussion on the SPIRIT-FILLED WALK.)

Acts 1:8
"But you shall receive <u>power</u> when the Holy Spirit has come upon you; and you shall be My witnesses both in Jerusalem, and in all Judea and Samaria, and even to the remotest part of the earth."

● What does the Holy Spirit give you? _____

● Should you witness without the Holy Spirit? _____

● Do you know why the Holy Spirit is so important?

_____

HERE IS WHAT JESUS SAID...

John 16:8
"And He (the Holy Spirit), when He comes, will convict the world concerning <u>sin</u>, and <u>righteousness</u>, and <u>judgment</u>."

•Who does the work of convicting?_____

•What does the Holy Spirit convict the world of?

_____

(Sin, righteousness, and judgment.)

When the Holy Spirit convicts the world of:

$IN =

This is the <u>sin</u> of unbelief; the Holy Spirit lets people know they need to believe in Jesus Christ as Saviour.

RIGHTEOUSNESS=

This is the righteousness of Jesus Christ; the Holy Spirit impresses upon the unbeliever the perfect <u>righteousness</u> of Jesus and His sacrifice for our sin.

JUDGMENT=

For those who reject Jesus Christ, the Holy Spirit will convict them of the <u>judgment</u> to come.

EFFECTIVE $HARING IS...

You need to realize that effective witnessing is <u>sharing</u> Jesus Christ, allowing the power of the Holy Spirit to convict the person with whom you are sharing. Remember that it is God who changes lives, not you.

C. You should be <u>familiar with the Scripture</u> to be and effective witness.

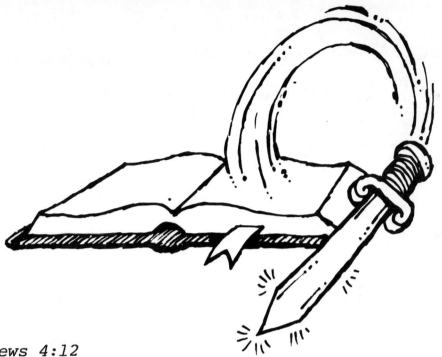

Hebrews 4:12
"For the word of God is _living_ and _active_ and _sharper than any two-edged sword_, piercing as far as the division of the soul and spirit, of both joints and marrow, and _able to judge the thoughts and intentions of the heart._"

● What are some characteristics of God's word? _____

_____

● What is God's word able to do?

_____

_____

(Please check out these other verses: I Thessalonians 2:13 and II Timothy 4:2)

D. You should pray for those whom you talk to about Jesus Christ, in order to be an effective and powerful witness.

II Peter 3:9
"The Lord is not slow about His promise, as some count slowness, but is patient toward you, _not wishing for any to perish but for all to come to repentance_."

●What does the Lord desire for all people? _____

_____

I John 5:14-15
"And this is the confidence which we have before Him, that, _if we ask anything according to His will_, _He hears us_. And if we know that He hears us in whatever we ask, _we know that we have the requests which we have asked from Him_."

●What is God's response if you pray according to His will? _____
(He hears you, and gives you your request.)

GOD'S PROMISE!

God promises that if you pray according to His will, He will hear and answer. We know from II Peter 3:9 that God's will is for no one to perish. Therefore, you can pray for your friends and parents, if they don't know God, that He'll use you to share the love and life of Jesus Christ. You can also expect results since you are praying according to God's will.

KEYS TO WITNESSING...
●Be Christ-centered

●Be Spirit-filled

●Be familiar with the Scripture

●Be prayerful and expectant

LET'S SUMMARIZE...

1. *Jesus calls you to proclaim the gospel.*

2. *Your message is to be centered around the Person of Jesus Christ -- His life, death & resurrection*

3. *Some practical things to remember in witnessing:*

- *Be Christ-centered*
- *Be Spirit-filled*
- *Be aware of the proper Scripture*
- *Be prayerful and expectant*

CAN YOU THINK OF SOMEONE?

Can you think of someone who does not know Jesus Christ? Will you begin to pray for this person, and be available to God so that He can use you to share His love? Remember to trust God with the results. You are just to share Jesus Christ and His great love in the power of the Holy Spirit, and leave any response by this person to God. And be sure to keep on praying in spite of your friend's outward reaction!

SHARING YOUR FAITH - Study #1

Let's study some of the "basic ingredients" of the
Gospel in detail. For each set of verses, think of
a title that describes what they are talking about.
The first one is done as an example.

Verses	Title
A. John 10:10; John 7: 37, 38	God's promise of a new, abundant life
B. Romans 3:23; Isaiah 53:6	
C. Romans 5:8; II Corinthians 5:10	
D. Romans 5:8; I Peter 2:24; I Peter 3:18	
E. Acts 2:37, 38; Acts 16:30, 31; Revelation 3:20	

Now, using these basic ingredients, write out your own
version of the Gospel using your own words, just as if
you were telling it to a friend who doesn't know a thing
about Christianity. Pull out a sheet of notebook paper
to write on and be sure to include all the major ingredients. You might also want to refer back to Discussion
10 in your manual.

You may wonder, "Where do I begin? Who should I witness to first?" God clearly provides a starting point in witnessing for every Christian. Let's find out who these special people are. Examine John 1:35-40. Who was the first person Andrew went to after he met Christ? What relation was this person to him?

_____

Do you have any brothers or sisters? Write down their names.

_____

Study Mark 5:1-20. Where did this man desire to be? Where did Jesus instruct him to go?

_____

_____

If Jesus were speaking to you in verse 19, who would He be sending you to? Write down several of their names.

_____

In light of these passages, who do you think God wants you to share the Good News with first?

_____

Look at the names you have written on this page. Now write down the two people you would most like to see accept Christ. Pray consistently for them each week, asking God for the right opportunity to share with them.

        1._____   2._____

We learn a new skill by studying how others do it and then practicing it. Sharing our faith is no exception. Today you will study the marvelous example of Jesus witnessing to the woman at the well. Carefully read John 4:1-30 and complete a PRESS and SPACE study (see discussion 5) on it. Here is a beautiful example of witnessing that demonstrates many principles involved in successfully communicating the Gospel. As you do the study, write down each principle you find illustrated in the passage that relates to witnessing.

_____

_____

_____

_____

_____

_____

_____

For a full discussion of this passage see the second chapter of Paul Little's book, How to Give Away Your Faith, published by Inter-Varsity Press.

"QUIET TIME HELPS" RELATED TO SHARING YOUR FAITH

WHAT THE QUIET TIME HELPS ARE ALL ABOUT

Every Christian needs to get quiet before God and take time to study the Bible--and worship God through prayer and praise.

After each discussion in this manual there are three "Quiet Time helps" which are designed to help you grow as a Christian.

It should take no more than a week for you to work your way through the three Quiet Time helps per discussion. After completing the three lessons you should sit down and discuss them with the person who is assisting you with the Discussion Manual for Student Discipleship.

SHARING YOUR FAITH QUIET TIME 1

Witnessing involves two things:

1. Who you are

2. What you say

It involves <u>who you are as a person</u>. You are one who has come to believe in and follow Jesus Christ. This aspect of witnessing entails your <u>conduct</u> - what you do as a person or your visual witness. Jesus spoke of this in Matthew 5:13-16.

What does He say concerning your visual witness? _____

_____

_____

This type of witness is seen <u>all</u> the time. It is reflected by your inner attitudes being lived out through your actions. The point is that you are a visual witness <u>all the time</u>! The question you need to ask yourself is, am I being a good witness or a poor witness to Jesus Christ?

What inner attitudes does Jesus say are important as we strive to be His witnesses through our conduct?

Luke 6:36-38 _____

_____

_____

Does John agree or disagree with Jesus' teaching?

I John 3:18 _____

You must realize that you have no right to give a verbal witness if your visual witness or conduct consistently and plainly contradicts all that Jesus taught.

As you follow Christ and build friendships with those around you, you will have an opportunity to share <u>a verbal witness for Christ</u>. This aspect of witnessing involves what you say about Jesus and how He has affected your life.

Verbal witness involves both the subjective and objective.

subjective witness - This is a simple statement of how Christ has changed you. It is your simple testimony. It does not necessarily contain a lot of Bible verses.

What was the blind man's subjective witness to the Pharisees?

John 9:1-25 _____

_____

_____

Write your own simple subjective testimony below:

_____

_____

_____

Every Christian can give a basic subjective witness. Every Christian should grow in their love and understanding of Christ so they can give an objective witness.

objective witness - This is a more detailed explanation of Christianity and how one can become a Christian. The "object" of your witness is Christ.

Write out a basic objective witness using the following three verses:

Romans 3:23 _____

_____

_____

_____

Romans 6:23 _____

_____

_____

_____

Romans 10:9, 10 _____

_____

_____

_____

What does I Peter 3:15 tell you about witnessing?

_____

_____

_____

SHARING YOUR FAITH QUIET TIME 2

Colossians 4:2-6 gives us three important principles to remember in witnessing.

They are: 1. You should be devoted to _____.

2. You should have wise _____.

3. You should have gracious _____.

DEVOTED TO PRAYER

Prayer for another shows that you have great concern and compassion for them.

What should be your motivation to pray?

Matthew 9:36-38 _____

_____

How did Paul express his concern for others that needed salvation?

Romans 10:1 _____

_____

CONDUCT SHOULD BE WISE

The following verses give some insight into wise conduct. List your thoughts after each verse:

Ephesians 5:15-16 _____

_____

_____

Ephesians 5:2 _____

_____

_____

186

Colossians 3:16 _____

_____

_____

Romans 12:18-21 _____

_____

_____

Matthew 10:16 _____

_____

_____

Proverbs 10:9, 11:3 _____

_____

_____

The Bible is filled with counsel concerning conduct. These verses were just a few to get you thinking. Write down the reasons why you feel wise conduct is important.

_____

_____

_____

GRACIOUS SPEECH

From the following verses, record your insights concerning gracious speech:

Proverbs 15:1 _____

_____

_____

Proverbs 16:24 _____

_____

_____

Ephesians 4:29 _____

_____

_____

Ephesians 4:25 _____

_____

_____

Ephesians 5:3-4 _____

_____

_____

Proverbs 10:19 _____

_____

_____

Proverbs 10:32 _____

_____

_____

What were Jesus' words like?

John 6:63, 68 _____

_____

_____

Why is it important to have gracious speech?

_____

_____

_____

_____

SHARING YOUR FAITH QUIET TIME 3
SUBJECT: A CRIPPLING ATTITUDE THAT HINDERS WITNESSING

What is this crippling attitude?

Proverbs 29:25 _____

_____

Being "afraid of man" brings a snare in two ways. Frist, it hinders people
from coming to Christ, and second, it slows down the Christian, because
rather than trusting and being obedient to God, he shrinks away from
sharing Christ because of his fear.

The cure for this fear is to see humanity from God's perspective. From the
following verses, list what God thinks of humanity.

Job 33:6 _____

_____

Psalms 103:14 _____

_____

Isaiah 40:22 _____

_____

James 1:10 _____

_____

James 4:4 _____

_____

What is the end of all humanity?

I Peter 4:3-5 _____

_____

_____

Even though you read these words, it is still difficult to get over fear. It seems that every time you have an opportunity to witness, fear runs through your heart. Don't let the fear prevent you from sharing, but **allow it to be a reminder that you need the help of the Holy Spirit as you share. Think of the fear as a "buzzer" reminding you to trust in the Lord.**

Also, try to get a feel for the temporary nature of your present activities. Realize that eternity is ahead and a very real hell exists where real people go. Answer the following questions, and this thought will become clearer.

Ten years from now will you remember or care about:

- The names of the ten smartest people in your graduating class?

- The girl with the nicest clothes?

- The guy who mocked you and made you afraid to stand up for God.

- The #1 athlete of the school?

- The guy with the hottest car? (If he's still alive!).

- The girl who got the most dates?

- The names of the four people in the clique that wouldn't be your friends?

- The score of the fifth game of the football season?

Write in your own words why it is wrong to fear the opinions of man over God.

_____

_____

_____

_____

_____

TODAY MORE THAN EVER BEFORE STUDENTS ARE ASKING THE QUESTIONS, — — "IS CHRISTIANITY PRACTICAL?" "WHAT WILL IT DO FOR ME?"

THE FOLLOWING SERIES OF MANUALS DEAL WITH GOD'S ANSWERS TO STUDENTS' NEEDS IN A PRACTICAL WAY.

Overhead Transparencies

for Volume I of the Discussion Manual for Student Relationships

You get . . .
- 78 Large Cartoon Pictures Right Out of the Manual
- Helpful Teaching Headlines
- Plenty of Space for Your Notes
- Colorful
- Reasonably Priced

Bring Visual Life to Your Teaching!
Let the Cartoons be a Teacher!
78 Transparencies for only $39.50!!

All 78 transparencies coordinate with the **Teacher's Guide** for optimum teaching effectiveness.

DISCUSSION MANUAL for STUDENT DISCIPLESHIP

WRITTEN BY
DAWSON McALLISTER
AND
JOHN MILLER

Volume 2

CHAPTER TITLE   DESCRIPTION

DiSCUSSiON MaNUaL for STUDENT. ReLaTioNSHiPS
Vol. 1

TEMPTATION
LONELINESS
DATING
PARENTS
SEX
LOVE

WRITTEN BY
JASON McLISTER
AND
DAN WEBSTER

CHaPTeR TiTLe   DeSCriPTioN

The Importance of Understanding ● ● The value and wisdom the Bible can shed
The Bible, A Counselling Book   on everyday life is discussed here.

The Importance of Knowing ● ● ● ● Whom should I marry? What school should
God's Will   I attend? What vocation should I pursue?
                                   are questions this chapter will help
                                   answer.

The Importance of a Balanced ● ● ● This chapter shares how God sees us and
Self-Image   how to form a proper self-image.

The Importance of Dealing ● ● ● ● One of the biggest problems the American st
with Loneliness   faces is loneliness. This chapter gives
                                   answers on how to deal with this problem.

The Importance of Understanding ● ● Few relationships affect our lives as do
Parents   our relationship with our parents. The
                                   problems and solutions are shared in
                                   this chapter.

The Importance of Understanding ● ● This section deals with the rationale of
Sex   why God's saying what He does about sex.

The Importance of Understanding ● ● This chapter gives insight into questions
Dating   such as--What are the problems in dating?
                                   What should I look for in a date? Does
                                   God have a plan for my date life?

The Importance of Understanding ● ● This work deals with some of the difference
Love   between love and infatuation.

The Importance of Clearing The ● ● The importance of thinking pure and Godly
Mind   thoughts are discussed in this chapter.

The Importance of Dealing With ● ● ● Being tempted and knowing who tempts us is
Temptation   not always easy to recognize. This
                                   chapter gives practical insights in the
                                   whole area of temptation.

The New TEACHER'S GUIDE

Makes the Discussion Manual

Easy and Complete to Teach!

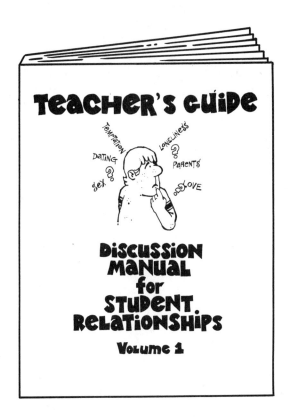

You Get:
- 26 Lessons in Outline Form
- Over 30 Projects
- Additional Bible References
- Hundreds of Questions
- Many Illustrations and Applications
- Lesson Aim and Goals
- Plus, Built-in Teacher Training Tips

Get this comprehensive TEACHER'S GUIDE today!

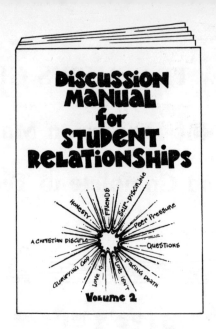

DISCUSSION MANUAL for STUDENT RELATIONSHIPS

Volume 2

Chapter Title

Description

This book is a must for the youth library.

DISCUSSION MANUAL for STUDENT RELATIONSHIPS

VOL. 3

CHAPTER TITLE

DESCRIPTION

How To Deal With Cliques • • • • This chapter deals with the ever common problem of cliques in a youth group, what God has to say about cliques and how to deal with bitterness toward the elite.

What To Do When Your Boyfriend Or Girlfriend "Drops You" • • • • Being rejected by someone we date and care about is very difficult to handle. This chapter relates to us dealing with broken hearts.

God's View Of The Misuse Of Drugs And Alcohol • • • • • • • This in depth discussion shares why God is absolutely against the misuse of drugs & alcohol. This work gives a positive answer to the problem -- the person of Jesus Christ.

How To Break Bad Habits • • • • Recognizing bad habits and learning how to break them is the topic of this chapter. Deep and practical truths are explained to the Christian on how to deal with sin.

How To Develop New Healthy Habits • This important section, in a very practical way, helps explain how to begin to form new and healthy habits.

How To Live In A Broken Home • • • Living in a broken home and allowing God's love to mend some of the hurts isn't easy. This chapter gives some insights into this area.

How To Deal With Guilt • • • • • Every student at one time or another faces the emotional pressure of guilt. This sections simply shares how God deals with guilt. This chapter is a must for any youth worker who does counseling.

The Christian Student And Rock Music • • • • • • • • The authors give insight into the advantages and disadvantages of listening to rock music and some creative alternatives.

Discipling Your Time • • • • • • Time is one of the most important commodities we have. This chapter deals with how to make the most of our time.

How to Face Death • • • • • • One thing we will all experience is death. This chapter answers the questions--What is death? Why is there death? Where does one go when he/she dies?